P9-DOH-858

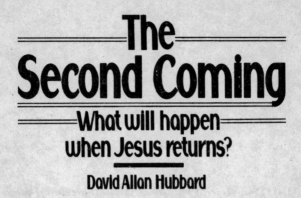

The Second Coming

What will happen when Jesus returns?

David Allan Hubbard

InterVarsity Press
Downers Grove
Illinois 60515

InterVarsity Press is the book-publishing division of Inter-Varsity Christian
Fellowship, a student movement active on campus at hundreds of
universities, colleges and schools of nursing. For information about local
and regional activities, write IVCF, 233 Langdon St., Madison, WI 53703.

Distributed in Canada through InterVarsity Press, 860 Denison St., Unit 3,
Markham, Ontario L3R 4H1, Canada.

Scripture quotations are from the Revised Standard Version of the Bible,
copyrighted 1946, 1952, © 1971, 1973.

Cover illustration: Roberta Polfus

ISBN 0-87784-968-4

Printed in the United States of America

Library of Congress Cataloging in Publication Data

Hubbard, David Allen.
  The second coming.

  1. Second Advent. 2. Eschatology. I. Title.
BT886.H83   1984   236   84-694
ISBN 0-87784-968-4

15	14	13	12	11	10	9	8	7	6	5	4	3	2	1
96	95	94	93	92	91	90	89	88	87	86	85	84		

Introduction

To a kid ten years old, many sermons seemed interminable, but the one that Sunday night threatened to set a longevity record—an hour and a half at least. The only thing that made it bearable was a huge chart, about thirty feet wide and ten feet high rigged like a schooner sail across the platform of my home church in Oakland, California. I guess the chart had a right to be huge. It plotted God's whole plan for history, from eternity to eternity.

As diverting as the chart was, it also posed a bit of a threat, because, as the speaker droned on, he talked without a single reference to the chart. The threat was obvious: if he had already exhausted an hour (not to speak of the congregation) without consulting the chart, how long could he keep going once he began to interpret it?

Happily, my father's tact, polished by forty years of ministry, saved us from answering that question. When the windy visitor announced "And now for the chart," my dad was ready with a counterannouncement: "Thank you, brother. We'll save the chart for another night."

Charts of the Times

Throughout my childhood there were other nights and other charts. The decade of the 1930s was ripe for them. The rise of Russia, the spreading empire of Mussolini, the menacing ambitions of Hitler—these and many other factors sent Christians scurrying to Bible studies and prophecy conferences to try to figure where history was headed and how the daily news could be fitted into God's plan for the ages.

Such questions were important to my mother, an ardent student and eloquent teacher of the Bible. My earliest childhood memories include sitting at her feet in various study groups as she quarried the books of Ezekiel, Daniel and Revelation for their wealth of insights about the future which God had in store for Israel and the church.

This was a good education. It built into me a confidence that history was headed for hope, that a sovereign God was in charge, that time was in short supply and needed to be used well and, above all, that the Jesus whom the apostles loved and followed and whom the Christians of all ages worshiped was actually, really, coming again.

What I missed—and this may have been as much my fault as my mother's—were the meaning and purpose of the grand events toward which God was nudging human history. Why a final judgment, a tribulation, a restoration of Israel, a millennium, two resurrections, a new heaven and earth? How do these components of Christ's second coming tie in with the other basic Christian affirmations like creation, the fall of humankind, the incarnation of Christ, the work of the Holy Spirit, the mission of the church?

Preoccupation with the sequence of events and concentration on the geography or schedule of the end times carry such fascination for us that we can easily neglect these more compelling questions. One purpose of this book, then, arises from my own pilgrimage. I have tried to think through for myself some implications of Christ's coming that were neglected in my earlier education.

If those devout studies of biblical prophecy on which I was raised (and which, to judge from book sales and Christian television programs, are enjoying a current revival) had any fault, it was to emphasize eschatology too little, not too much. Eschatology, biblical interpretation of last things, end-time events, has often been seen as merely the final chapter in God's redemptive program. It's much more. It is the North Star from which theological study gains its bearings, the giant floodlight by which God brightens the whole landscape of human life and history, the clearest picture we possess of what God really wants, what our place is in his plan, and what power he has to make all creation serve his glory.

Incentive for Today

The descriptions of Christ's second coming are intended not only to inform us of the future but to equip us for the present. The scenes of worship around the throne remind us that our ultimate behavior—ascribing glory and honor to the Lord and the Lamb—is to be our interim practice, so we gather regularly with God's people to praise him "from whom all blessings flow."

The assurance, granted so firmly in the Revelation, that Christ's church is finally united is our strongest incentive to work for Christian unity in the face of our dividedness. Neither history nor sociology can present us with a true vision of the oneness of God's people. Eschatology can.

The landscapes of the Bible's future are not polluted with the sights of injustice, the sounds of war or the pangs of deprivation. Peace, righteousness and plenty dwell there as celebrated achievements of the King of kings. It is the ethical perfection of that kingdom which both prods and guides us to get on with the task of loving our neighbors, living as peacemakers and offering the cups of cold water in the Savior's name. Christian ethics flow from our view of the future: we not only pray for God's will to be done on earth as it is in heaven, but we work to be part of the answer to that prayer.

This book may not have the detailed precision of my boyhood charts. It does exhibit, I trust, something of the same confidence in and excitement for the Second Coming that they sought to spark. If it can add theological understanding of God's purposes and personal motivation to cooperate with those purposes in our generation, it will have done what I intended. Assurance of God's purpose then and obedience to his purpose now, in light of that assurance, are the twin reasons for the Bible's talk about the future. No Christian dare have one without the other.

*But of that day or that hour no one knows, not even
the angels in heaven, nor the Son, but only the Father. Take heed, watch; for you do not know when the
time will come. It is like a man going on a journey,
when he leaves home and puts his servants in charge,
each with his work, and commands the doorkeeper to
be on the watch. Watch therefore—for you do not know
when the master of the house will come, in the evening,
or at midnight, or at cockcrow, or in the morning—lest
he come suddenly and find you asleep. And what I say
to you I say to all: Watch.*
Mark 13:32-37

I

The Certainty
of the
Second Coming

FOR REASONS THAT WE cannot quite understand, some historical events drop a noose around our minds and tie us to them. The war between France and England does that to me. Its heroes seem larger than life—Napoleon, Wellington, Nelson. Its battles were landmarks in the history of freedom—Waterloo and Trafalgar. Our history as English-speaking people would have been altered drastically had their outcome been different. The British won, and the marks of that victory are found in the monuments of almost every city in the United Kingdom, and in the consciousness of every British citizen. For the rest of us who speak English anywhere in the world, the word *Waterloo* has become a symbol of defeat, as Napoleon, Europe's proudest general, saw his army shattered and his empire eclipsed.

You too have special memories, memories of events you witnessed in person or in spirit. One generation of you marched on the sands of the French coast with Eisenhower's troops at D-Day, in those tides that sought to wash Europe of the Nazi scourge. Others of you may have joined John F. Kennedy on the inaugural stand when he challenged all Americans to "ask not what your country can do for you, but what you can do for your country." Still others of you rejoiced in the quest for justice and peace as you walked with Martin Luther King, Jr., from Selma to Montgomery or watched Begin and Sadat embrace after the Camp David meetings. Maybe you soared with Sally Ride and celebrated her contribution as the first American woman to venture into space.

Favorite events, memorable occasions, captivating episodes in history—all of these have two things in common. They happened in the past, and they happened at an hour we can mark on a calendar. They differ in both ways from history's grandest event. It is yet to come, and its hour is unknown. For those two reasons, in fact, we are tempted to treat it not as history, not as a concrete event. Yet that would be wrong.

The Second Coming was certainly high on Jesus' list. Whole sections of his teaching were devoted to it. "Of that day or that hour no one knows," he said, "not even the angels in heaven, nor the Son, but only the Father. Take heed, watch; for you do not know when the time will come" (Mk 13:32-33).

These words of Jesus trigger three questions. First, how can we be sure Christ will come back? The event seems so remote, so unlikely. Second, how should we react? We are tempted to respond at times in panic and at other times in apathy; what kind of attitude should knowledge of his return create in us? And, third, how can we get ready? It is hard to prepare for an event that we cannot schedule. Yet Jesus' command to us is "Watch!" How to do that is our prime concern in this study.

Its Certainty

Jesus' second coming is a historical event. Its fact is certain, though its time is unknown. These realities are hard for us to grasp. History past we can have reasonable confidence in. We can visit the battlefield at Waterloo and walk around the great mound where many of the dead are buried. We can hear on tape the New England accent and the steely voice of President Kennedy. We can watch replays on television of the reconciliation of Sadat and Begin.

But the Second Coming, whose hour we cannot know—that seems like a different matter. How can we be sure?

God's Word teaches it: that is the first evidence of its certainty. The same book that tells us of the wonders of God's creation, the miracle of Christ's incarnation and the mysteries of the Holy Spirit informs us that God has yet one other great work to do.

15

We can trust the Bible. Its predictions in the past have come true; think of the promises of Jesus' *first* coming. Its analyses of our human condition have proved right; think what it tells us about ourselves. Its power to apply its truths has been demonstrated; think how our lives have been transformed by what it told us. We can trust God's Word even when Christ's coming seems incredibly slow.

We can be sure Christ will come because God's plan demands it. That is the second evidence. Jesus told us God's plan in the prayer he taught his followers: "Thy will be done, On earth as it is in heaven" (Mt 6:10).

One look at our history, our civilization, our society and our own lives will tell us how far that prayer is from fulfillment. Nor is a human remedy in sight. No human agency—not our governments, not the United Nations, not the ecumenical movement, not even our evangelical churches—can bring that prayer to pass. Only God can do that. And his final means will be Christ's coming. All that God intended when he first created will be brought about in history's last, best adventure. We can trust God's plan even when Christ's coming seems unbelievably far away.

We can be sure Christ will come because his resurrection guarantees it. Paul's sermon to the Greeks in Athens needs to be heard by us all: God "commands all men everywhere to repent, because he has fixed a day on which he will judge the world in righteousness by a man whom he has appointed, and of this he has given assurance to all men by raising him from the dead" (Acts 17:30-31). Does

Jesus' coming seem uncertain, delayed, postponed almost to the point of cancellation? Take another look at the empty tomb. Let every day be Easter. Christ has risen from the dead; the power of God has done the impossible. The living Christ is ready to break into earth's history once more. We can trust Christ's resurrection, even when doubt and death seem to hang huge shadows over God's promises.

God's Word, his plan to do his will on earth, and the victorious resurrection of Jesus all reassure us that Christ's coming is at least as certain as Napoleon's defeat. How we react to that certainty makes all the difference.

Our Response

No sensible person, confronted with the reality of Jesus' triumphant return, can yawn or turn the page. It is the climax of all that human life has been heading toward. It is the wonder of a thousand Christmases, Easters, Fourth of Julys and Thanksgiving Days rolled into one. Apathy is incomprehensible. That is why Christ's words were "Take heed, watch."

But panic is no better a response than apathy. The date is in God's hands. History will roll forward at his pace; the end will come at his time. We do not sell all our goods and don white robes as some believers did. We do not rush to the hilltops to wait as some Christians have. We do not spend frenzied effort trying to chart the time as some of God's people do.

No, we react with a sense of trust. Who knows

the time? Not the angels in their creatureliness; not the Son in his humble, earthly dependence on the Father. Who knows the time? The Father does—the loving Father, whose concern is for our well-being; the wise Father, whose decisions are always right; the powerful Father, whose plans can never fail. The timing is in good hands. We can live with our anxieties; we can handle our doubts. God has fixed the day. No force in earth or hell can unfix it. That is reassuring.

We also react with a sense of rededication. That was the point of Jesus' insistence that his people be on the watch. His illustration went like this: "It is like a man going on a journey, when he leaves home and puts his servants in charge, each with his work, and commands the doorkeeper to be on the watch. Watch therefore—for you do not know when the master of the house will come, in the evening, or at midnight, or at cockcrow, or in the morning—lest he come suddenly and find you asleep" (Mk 13:34-36).

Confidence, of course, was one possible reaction. The master was coming. They had his word on it. Vigilance was another. They did not know when he would come. Their servanthood called for deep commitment just because they did not know. They had to be diligent when the master was at home, and they had to be just as diligent while he was away. At any moment he could return and call them to account for the quality of their service.

The doorkeeper especially was on the spot. His task was to hear the master's call, open the gate, care for his cloak, wash his feet and ease the burden of his journey. His was the privilege of first welcome. He had the joy of seeing the master first. He also had the duty of being constantly ready. Christ has called all of his people to be gatekeepers, watchful and joyful. "Watch, therefore": history's grandest happening is on the way.

Our Readiness

"What I say to you I say to all: Watch" (Mk 13:37). With those words of summation Jesus made sure that none of us could dodge his command. Because we know the certainty of that hour but not its timing, watchfulness, readiness, is to be our duty.

What does readiness entail? Watch, Jesus ordered. But how? First, we must establish our relationship with the Father. It is to the Father's servants that Jesus will come with joy and blessing. We must make sure that we belong. Have we acknowledged that we cannot live without God? Have we rejected our godless independence? Have we turned from our selfishness and arrogance? Have we said yes to the Father's call to come home and be part of his family? Christ's coming is sure; the hour is not. That combination spurs us to trust him for salvation and guidance.

Second, we must alert our loved ones to history's destiny. They can learn nothing about this from history books or news media. History's most important lessons are not to be found there. Christian watchfulness always includes calling others to watch with us. God has revealed to us the secrets of his future, but they are not to be kept secret. They are to be shared with all our loved ones, broadcast to all who know us. The Master is coming back to the world for which he died. That message is history's most significant announcement.

Third, we must pursue our calling with enthusiasm. That too is part of the command to watch. The servants are in charge, Jesus stated, "each with his work."

Each of us knows best what the calling involves. It may be to care for an aged loved one, to raise children to love the Lord, to be an excellent carpenter, to translate the Bible into a tribal language, to bring good cheer to a lonely neighbor. We must do what we are called to do with eagerness. The Master is on his way back. He looks forward to rewarding our faithfulness.

The certainty of Christ's return has a purifying effect on his people. "And every one who thus hopes in him purifies himself as he is pure" (1 Jn 3:3). What needs to be set in order in our lives as we watch for the great surprise? A bill to be paid? An apology to be offered? A word of Christian witness to be spoken? A broken relationship to be mended? We dare not put it off. Christ is on the way. He wants his people ready.

History is headed toward his day. The great victories are yet to be won. Beside them Waterloo, Trafalgar, D-Day and Camp David will look like children's games. That future is our anchor and hope. We do not know its *when*. We do know its *Who*. It is the Father's day. He knows. And we know that he knows. That is all we need to know. Now we can get on with our watching.

But we would not have you ignorant, brethren, concerning those who are asleep, that you may not grieve as others do who have no hope. For since we believe that Jesus died and rose again, even so, through Jesus, God will bring with him those who have fallen asleep. For this we declare to you by the word of the Lord, that we who are alive, who are left until the coming of the Lord, shall not precede those who have fallen asleep. For the Lord himself will descend from heaven with a cry of command, with the archangel's call, and with the sound of the trumpet of God. And the dead in Christ will rise first; then we who are alive, who are left, shall be caught up together with them in the clouds to meet the Lord in the air; and so we shall always be with the Lord. Therefore comfort one another with these words.

1 Thessalonians 4:13-18

2

The Purpose of Christ's Coming

THERE CAN BE NO doubt as to our curiosity about the universe beyond us. The shelves of our bookstores are lined with volumes on science fiction. A major airline announced a waiting list for its first trip to the moon and found the list full, even though no date was in sight. Television series like *Star Trek* that have specialized in space travel have ensnared whole cults of devotees. And two of the most popular movies in history have purported to disclose the secrets of the worlds beyond our world.

People who saw the first episode of *Star Wars* reported a fascinating phenomenon. After all the suspense and intrigue had come to a head, after the forces of good had destroyed the home of the hosts of evil and Darth Vadar, their heinous leader, the audience in the theaters burst out in gales of cheering and applause. They wanted righteousness to be the final victor, and their appreciation when it happened knew no bounds.

Close Encounters of the Third Kind carried another message, equally welcome. It alerted its viewers to life on other planets. It pictured visitations from beyond to our world. It grasped the attention of millions of lonely passengers on spaceship earth and told them that they were not alone.

The messages of these films are precisely what we long to hear. They speak to our sense of defeatism and alienation. They bring hope to a world bleak with despair over the power of evil and the horror of isolation. With stereophonic sound and technicolor film, they placard their twin slogans: "Righteousness will win" and "We are not alone."

It is strange that people all over the world find in films the assurance that they have overlooked in the Bible. Far more intriguing than galactic wars, far more thrilling than space travel, is the Bible's picture of God's future. At its center is the description of Christ's personal return. From worlds beyond he ventures forth to revisit our planet and to claim it as his conquered territory.

From the beginning this climactic event has stood at the heart of Christian preaching. Jesus himself announced it: "And then they will see the Son of man coming in clouds with great power and glory" (Mk 13:26). The white-robed heralds who attended Christ's ascension looked forward to that

24

next great day: "This Jesus, who was taken up from you into heaven, will come in the same way as you saw him go into heaven" (Acts 1:11). Wherever the apostles preached, the reality of this announcement was held before their hearers. Jesus' lordship, his perfection, his death and resurrection, his ascension and return: these were the central themes of the Christian message. Repentance and faith were the only proper responses to a Christ of such power and glory.

Any uncertainty that the Jews and Gentiles suffered about the future was dispelled by a picture of victory and fellowship. "Righteousness will win" and "You will not be left alone." These assurances were as encouraging to ancient audiences as they are to us. Even more so, because the Bible version is grounded in the reality of God's history, not in the fiction of a scientist's imagination.

The Glory of the Victory

Christ's promise to return and the apostles' repetition of that promise led many Christians in the first century to believe that Jesus would come back in their lifetime. This belief spawned a degree of uncertainty. Persecution and financial hardship cut short the lives of some believers. With sadness and anxiety their Christian loved ones laid them to rest. Would they ever see them alive again? Would the dead be able to enjoy the celebration when the Lord returned? Or would their death so defeat them that they would not share Christ's victory?

To answer such questions, Paul wrote his loved

ones in Thessalonica. With glowing affirmations he assuaged their uncertainty: "We would not have you ignorant, brethren, concerning those who are asleep, that you may not grieve as others do who have no hope. For since we believe that Jesus died and rose again, even so, through Jesus, God will bring with him those who have fallen asleep" (1 Thess 4:13-14).

We cannot miss the notes of glory in this chronicle of victory yet to come. The victory is glorious because of what is conquered: *death*. Death has a viciously effective way of looking like a winner, whether by slow destruction or lightning attack.

When old age sets in, or irreversible disease, death seems unconquerable. With relentless steps it shrivels the body, erodes the mind and enfeebles the spirit. As the years go by or the cancer eats away, we watch a person shrink into a frightful shell. Inch by inch humanity seems to fade and disappear before our eyes. Death has all the marks of a winner.

Death can also surprise by quick invasion. The brakes screech; tires skid; metal grinds; glass crumbles. One minute a college girl is radiant with laughter at her boyfriend's side; the next minute she is lying laughless on the pavement, her life snuffed out with the snap of her neck. Death seems to have won again.

Yet Paul's words about Jesus' coming tell us that death is conquered, conquered so thoroughly that it can be called sleep, conquered so finally that the whole nature of grieving is changed. Grieving is lifted by hope, not drowned in hopelessness.

It is a glorious victory because death is the victim. The seeming winner has become the certain loser.

With the defeat of death, a whole lot of other enemies bite the dust. Behind death lurks sin, which had caused the terror of death in the first place. The defeat of death means defeat for sin, which has used death as its wages through the centuries. And behind sin stands the plot of Satan to keep us from loving God and serving his purposes. The defeat of death means the defeat of sin, which means the defeat of Satan. Like dominoes they go down, these dastardly enemies. Christ's victory is glorious because of what is conquered.

The victory is also glorious because of how the conquest is gained. It is a victory gained by love and power: "For since we believe that Jesus died and rose again . . ." The love that led Jesus to the cross and the power that brought him back from the dead are on our side. Not brute power, so cruel and heartless, not impotent love, so weak and inept, but loving power and powerful love. These are the weapons which God uses to bring the final victory. They can be counted on to win, and to do so winsomely.

Most important, the victory is glorious because of who the Conqueror is. "God will bring with him those who have fallen asleep." What God does, he does to perfection. What he created at the beginning he could call good. His conquest at the end he will also call good. His is the power to change death to sleep, so harmless has it become; his is the power to snatch the sting from grief, so great is the hope he gives; his is the power to bring with Jesus all the dead believers, so abundant is the life that he engenders.

One great purpose, then, of Christ's coming is to reveal God's glory and power by winning a smashing victory over all our human enemies. It is a victory which only God can win. It is a victory which God will surely win. If audiences in theaters around the world can explode in applause for the victors in *Star Wars*, God's people ought to raise the roofs of home and church when we think of Christ's second coming.

The Wonder of the Fellowship

The glory of the victory is matched by the wonder of the fellowship. Death is the great separator. It cuts us off from those whom we most love and need.

Paul's friends at Thessalonica thought death might separate them permanently from their loved ones. Worse still, they feared that death would separate their loved ones from Christ. Paul laid both those fears to rest as he described the ultimate fellowship that all God's people will enjoy at Christ's coming:

> For this we declare to you by the word of the Lord, that we who are alive, who are left until the coming of the Lord, shall not precede those who have fallen asleep. For the Lord himself will descend from heaven with a cry of command, with the archangel's call, and with the sound of the trumpet of God. And the dead in Christ will rise first; then we who are alive, who are left,

shall be caught up together with them in the
clouds to meet the Lord in the air; and so we shall
always be with the Lord. (1 Thess 4:15-17)

The fellowship is wonderful in its results. Reunion,
not separation, is the theme. The Christian dead
will not be cut out of the Second Coming with its
joy and celebration. They will lead the parade of
resurrection. They rise first, roused from death by
the powerful descent of Christ.

The fellowship is wonderful in its setting. The
cry of command, the archangel's call, the trumpet
blast—all these signal the irresistible power of
God. Like a general in full military array he invades
our dying planet and infuses it with resurrection
life.

Fellowship, not separation, is God's will and
God's gift. Living believers and the resurrected
dead meet each other in the air. The oneness of
God's people is experienced afresh.

The fellowship is wonderful in its permanence.
With death, sin, sorrow and Satan all defeated, no
further enemies remain. No barriers can be erected
to divide Christian from Christian or Christians
from their Lord: "And so we shall always be with
the Lord."

The fellowship is wonderful in its perfection. It
is the Lord with whom God's people are reunited.
No fellowship can compare with that. It is the Garden of Eden revisited and more. Harmony with
God's will, obedience to God's purposes, enjoy-
ment of God's person—these strands are woven
together in the bond of fellowship: "And so we
shall always be with the *Lord*."

29

The purpose of Christ's coming, then, is not to satisfy our curiosity or enhance our importance. It is to fulfill God's ancient plan, his plan to display his glory and to enjoy the love of his people.

These thoughts bring hope and comfort as we look forward. As Paul wrote, we may "comfort one another with these words" (1 Thess 4:18). Understanding God's purposes for the future can help us find purpose in the present. Light from tomorrow can dispel darkness today. Righteousness can win now as well as then, as we seek God's grace and strength. He is just as powerful now as he ever will be. Separation, loneliness and division can be defeated now as they will be when the Conqueror comes. God is with us already, longing to bind his people together and to encourage us by his presence.

The victory and the fellowship which movie audiences have responded to in *Star Wars* and *Close Encounters* are available to all God's people. We can count on him to do all that we need, at Christ's coming and now.

So when you see the desolating sacrilege spoken of by the prophet Daniel, standing in the holy place (let the reader understand), then let those who are in Judea flee to the mountains; let him who is on the housetop not go down to take what is in his house; and let him who is in the field not turn back to take his mantle. And alas for those who are with child and for those who give suck in those days! Pray that your flight may not be in winter or on a sabbath. For then there will be great tribulation, such as has not been from the beginning of the world until now, no, and never will be. And if those days had not been shortened, no human being would be saved; but for the sake of the elect those days will be shortened.

Matthew 24:15-22

3

The
Great
Tribulation

THE HEADLINES HOWL with anguish. It makes us feel faint to read them. They seem to fling themselves at us from around the globe. PASTORS IMPRISONED IN SOUTH KOREA FOR OPPOSING GOVERNMENT POLICY. PRIESTS HELD INCOMMUNICADO IN ARGENTINA. NUNS ACCUSED OF REVOLUTIONARY TACTICS IN GUATEMALA. SOVIET COURT SENTENCES BAPTIST PREACHER TO TEN YEARS IN LABOR CAMP. ARCHBISHOP SLAIN IN UGANDA. ENGLISH PENTECOSTALS SLAUGHTERED IN ZIMBABWE.

At times the world seems infested with religious

persecution. Like a great plague the infection spreads from country to country. At times life for God's people seems like a continual wake, so blanketed is the world with hostility toward the worship and service of God.

We should dread it, shun it, hate it. But we should not be surprised by it. Persecution was to be as constant a companion of Christ's followers as the Holy Spirit who dwells with us and in us. In fact, when Jesus promised the Spirit as Comforter, he also promised struggle as a way of life: "In the world you have tribulation; but be of good cheer, I have overcome the world" (Jn 16:33). The good cheer we can speak of later; for now our attention is on the tribulation which is part of our life in the world.

What is it? How do we distinguish tribulation from other forms of suffering? Tribulation is not suffering that we bring on ourselves. The alcoholic cannot describe the hardening of his liver as persecution. The lecherous man cannot blame the devil for his venereal disease. In cirrhosis of the liver or syphilis, there is plenty of suffering—and eventually death. But they cannot be called tribulation.

Nor is tribulation the suffering we undergo when God's creation seems to turn wild. Flood, drought, hurricane and earthquake can all inflict unbearable hardship and destruction. We pray to God that they will not happen and cry for relief when they do. But they are not what the Bible describes as tribulation.

Tribulation is not the suffering that comes our way in the normal course of human carelessness.

Sinners that we are, we hurt others and get hurt ourselves. Harsh words, mean looks, dirty tricks, cruel deeds—these are our stock-in-trade as fallen rebels. The amount of pain unleashed by such carelessness is monumental. Children neglect their aged parents, distraught wives frustrate their husbands, hostile husbands abuse their wives, neighbors ignore each other or gossip and lie about each other. Bitter, hurtful stuff, all of it. But this is not tribulation.

What then is tribulation, as the Bible describes it? It is the experiences of pressure and persecution that God's people endure at the hands of those who oppose his program of salvation. Tribulation is the opposition and oppression that the political, economic, social and religious leaders of the world bring to bear on those who call Jesus Lord, just because they do call Jesus Lord.

Tribulation is part of the lot of God's people in a world whose values are shaped by Satan. It may vary in intensity from era to era, but it has almost always been present to harry the church of Christ somewhere in the world, just as Jesus promised.

We know from Scripture that the intensity of Satan's effort to turn people against God will increase just before Christ comes again. In fact, that period of tribulation, usually called the Great Tribulation, is a vitally important part of the context of the Second Coming (Rev 7:14). Painful as the subject is, the Great Tribulation must be understood if we are to wait eagerly for Christ's return and if we are to understand what we are waiting for. The headlines are full of anguish now as

Christ's followers undergo persecution. Yet, by Christ's own word, matters are to get far worse before he comes: "Then there will be great tribulation, such as has not been from the beginning of the world until now, no, and never will be" (Mt 24:21).

When will it come? Why will it happen? What will it be like? How do we get ready? These are the questions that we must deal with to grasp the meaning of the Great Tribulation and the bearing it has on history's close.

When Will It Come?

We cannot put a date on the tribulation. Its timing, like the hour of Christ's coming, is hidden in the mysteries of God. Scripture does, however, tell us two things about its timing.

First, the tribulation will come just before our Lord returns. Here is Jesus' explanation:

Immediately after the tribulation of those days the sun will be darkened, and the moon will not give its light, and the stars will fall from heaven, and the powers of the heavens will be shaken; then will appear the sign of the Son of man in heaven, and then all the tribes of the earth will mourn, and they will see the Son of man coming on the clouds of heaven with power and great glory; and he will send out his angels with a loud trumpet call, and they will gather his elect from the four winds, from one end of heaven to the other. (Mt 24:29-31)

The tribulation is the last significant period of human history immediately prior to the glorious appearing of Jesus Christ. The length of that period is not fully clear from Scripture, although there is some indication that it may last seven years. Part of the uncertainty has to do with the interpretation of the number *seven*, which may have either a literal or a symbolic meaning. It often symbolizes fullness or completeness. Hence its meaning in relationship to the tribulation could be a period of time long enough for the turmoil and testing of Satan's hosts to do their full work.

The second thing to be understood about the timing is that we will know the Great Tribulation has arrived when the antichrist appears (2 Thess 2:1-12). Persecution in biblical history is virtually always connected with an evil, influential leader. Pharaoh afflicted the Israelites in Egypt; Nebuchadnezzar hauled the citizens of Judah away to Babylon; Haman plotted their death in the days of Esther; Antiochus Epiphanes forced his pagan ways on them from 171 to 165 B.C.; Titus, the Roman general, ravaged Jerusalem in A.D. 70, after Nero had ordered the deaths of Peter and Paul. So goes the pattern.

At the end of history a vicious and powerful ruler, called "a beast," will arise (Rev 13:1). Satan will give him authority and power. For a period of three and one-half years he will ravage the people of God, exercise dictatorial powers over the earth and demand to be worshiped in the place of the true and living God (Rev 13:1-10).

The appearance of this beast, this political-economic-religious dictator, is the clearest mark of the tribulation. No wonder John concluded his description of the beast's savagery with these words: "Here is a call for the endurance and faith of the saints" (Rev 13:10)!

Why Will It Happen?

Probably a more pressing question than *when* is *why*. What purposes can God have in mind to allow such a brutal experience to batter the world he has made and the people he loves?

God's first purpose in the Great Tribulation is to display his wrath. Like the flood in Noah's day, the tribulation will see a deluge of judgment on those who have failed to love God as God and to walk in his ways. As always, God's punishment will be directly related to the nature of the crime. What has been the world's desire but to ignore God and to deify humanity? And what has been the world's pattern but to heed the voice of Satan rather than the call of God?

What the world has desired throughout the millenniums of history God will give it in lavish measure at the end. Pharaoh hardened his heart against God's command in the days of Israel's captivity; he deliberately set his will against God's and would not release God's people. God then gave Pharaoh what Pharaoh wanted, a heart so hard that he could not change his mind. He resisted God to the end and was punished accordingly. Similarly, the tribulation will be God's way of giving people what they asked for: the rule of Satan in lavish measure. God can give no greater judgment than to let godless people have their own way.

God's second purpose in allowing the tribulation is to test his people. Like Job we shall be asked to show that we love God in the midst of hardship and deprivation. Like Daniel we shall be asked to obey God rather than godless rulers. Like Jesus himself, we may be asked to commend our spirits to God when our persecutors do us in.

Jesus is Lord! That is our basic Christian affirmation. The tribulation will, for God's people, be history's greatest opportunity to prove we really believe that. As our brothers and sisters in the early church were pinned to the cross or bound to the stake because they would not pledge their final allegiance to Caesars like Nero, Domitian or Diocletian, so their counterparts at the end will be martyred because they refuse to bow to antichrist. Jesus, not a government nor a governor, is Lord. That is the great lesson which God's people will spell out in their blood just before the Savior returns.

What Will It Be Like?

The conflict between the lordship of Jesus and the authority of antichrist reminds us that one feature of the tribulation will be its totalitarian structure. A rigid rule will be set up that will regulate every area of life, especially commercial life. No buying or selling will be allowed except by the license of antichrist.

The totalitarian structure will promote a blasphemous religious system. Men and women will be forced to worship the beast, as the antichrist is fittingly branded. He will set himself up as god in the temple of God. This is idolatry at its emptiest,

blasphemy at its baldest. History's worst villain—
Atilla the Hun, Hitler and Stalin rolled into one—
will demand that men and women adore his name
instead of that of the Most High God, the righteous
Lord of heaven and earth.

The implications of all of this for God's people
are ferocious, an unprecedented persecution.
Hosts of true worshipers will lay down their lives
—and that after years of harassment and deprivation. No wonder Christ said this period was so
fierce that God had to shorten it for the sake of his
chosen ones!

How Do We Get Ready?

To be forewarned is to be forearmed: the old prov-
erb never had a better application. The Bible tells
us about the tribulation so that, if we are asked by
God to go through it, we can be ready. How?

First, be aware of the way evil works. We are
tempted by fiction and drama to view Satan's work
as mystical or magic, full of evil spells and menacing omens. That may be the case at times, but it is
not usually. Satan is much more apt to work
through wicked governments and their leaders.
Organized evil is much more to be dreaded than
disorganized evil. We must, therefore, always have
an eye on what governments are doing to throttle
human rights or to resist the authority of God.

Second, be alert to the meaning of Christ's lordship. In the small choices of life we must learn to
put him first. This will keep us in training in case
the big choice comes—the choice between the command of a beastly government and the demand that

we be loyal to Jesus our Lord.

Finally, be assured of the powerful love of God. Who guarded Israel in Egyptian slavery? Who preserved Daniel in Babylonian captivity? Who saw Job through to health and prosperity? Who brought Jesus back from the dead? Who used the martyrs' blood to plant the church? The powerful love of God has seen and will see his people through.

The headlines howl now with anguish as God's people endure tribulation. They foreshadow the vicious headlines yet to come. We read them soberly, yet with hope. Through them God calls us to be ready for whatever happens and reminds us that Christ is able to see us through.

There was a rich man, who was clothed in purple and fine linen and who feasted sumptuously every day. And at his gate lay a poor man named Lazarus, full of sores, who desired to be fed with what fell from the rich man's table; moreover the dogs came and licked his sores. The poor man died and was carried by the angels to Abraham's bosom. The rich man also died and was buried; and in Hades, being in torment, he lifted up his eyes, and saw Abraham far off and Lazarus in his bosom. And he called out, "Father Abraham, have mercy upon me, and send Lazarus to dip the end of his finger in water and cool my tongue; for I am in anguish in this flame." But Abraham said, "Son, remember that you in your lifetime received your good things, and Lazarus in like manner evil things; but now he is comforted here, and you are in anguish. And besides all this, between us and you a great chasm has been fixed, in order that those who would pass from here to you may not be able, and none may cross from there to us." And he said, "Then I beg you, father, to send him to my father's house, for I have five brothers, so that he may warn them, lest they also come into this place of torment." But Abraham said, "They have Moses and the prophets; let them hear them." And he said, "No, father Abraham; but if some one goes to them from the dead, they will repent." He said to him, "If they do not hear Moses and the prophets, neither will they be convinced if some one should rise from the dead."
Luke 16:19-31

4

Heaven
and
Hell

THE LANDSCAPE OF ancient Israel must have looked strange to a visiting caravaner from Egypt. Splashing buckets of water into the troughs at the oasis, a camel driver might well have scanned the horizon looking for the architectural symbols most familiar to him: "What kind of land is this? I have traveled its length from Beersheba to Dan and have seen no pyramid, no massive monumental tomb like those that cast such colossal shadows across the plains of Gizeh."

If anyone had answered the puzzled Egyptian, he would have become even more confused, for the burial customs of God's people stood in sharp con-

trast to those of Egypt. The Israelites did not em-
balm their dead nor place them in decorated cof-
fins. The bodies were simply wrapped and laid in
caves or tombs hewn out of the rugged hillsides.
Neither food nor personal possessions were buried
with them. In fact, death was viewed as unclean-
ness, and the household in which death had taken
place had to undergo special rites of purification.

Israel's attitude toward death was directly
shaped by its understanding of God. God alone
was fully sovereign over all of life, so no cult of
the dead could be fostered. Dead kings were no
more to be deified or idolized than were living
kings. They were buried with dignity in hillside
tombs, but they were not especially revered after
death. Nor were their spirits feared in such a way
that magical ceremonies had to be practiced to keep
them from harming the living.

For the Israelites God alone was truly living, un-
touchable by death, decay or destruction. Human
life was his gift, totally subject to his power. No
view of afterlife could be tolerated that suggested
that humankind had independent existence that
continued regardless of God's purpose and power.

So Israel's sights were focused by God on the
here and now. Worship of God, reverence for his
work in history, regard for his laws of love and
justice—these were the occupations of God's ancient people, not speculations about life after
death. When they did talk about it, they used the
term *Sheol* to describe a gray, half-alive place where
the dead existed cut off from the life of the world
and the Lord who gave that world life. Here is Job's

gloomy description of Sheol, the abode of the dead:

Are not the days of my life few?
Let me alone, that I may find a little comfort
before I go whence I shall not return,
to the land of gloom and deep darkness,
the land of gloom and chaos,
where light is as darkness. (Job 10:20-22)

The clearest clue as to the difference the Israelites saw between life and death comes from Hezekiah's prayer for healing:

For Sheol cannot thank thee,
death cannot praise thee;
those who go down to the pit cannot hope
for thy faithfulness.
The living, the living, he thanks thee,
as I do this day;
the father makes known to the children
thy faithfulness. (Is 38:18-19)

What was Sheol? The place where people could not praise God and witness to his faithfulness. What was it to be alive? It was to gather with God's people to celebrate the glories of his name. Life was relationship with God and the opportunity to praise him. Death was the lack of that relationship and that opportunity.

As God revealed more truth about himself to his people and as they experienced his sovereignty and his life, the spiritual leaders of Israel realized that their understanding of Sheol was not the whole story. Something more awaited them after death.

For one thing, their fellowship with God was so rich that they could not believe that death could dampen it. They knew that the living God was with them continually in life and that he was larger than death:

> Nevertheless I am continually with thee;
>> thou dost hold my right hand.
> Thou dost guide me with thy counsel,
>> and afterward thou wilt receive me to glory.
> (Ps 73:23-24)

For another thing, the sovereign God did not always carry out his judgment on the living. Wicked people died prosperous, without full punishment for their godlessness. Righteous people died prematurely in tragic accidents, unrewarded for their faith and devotion. Yet the sovereign Judge of all the earth had to do right. How could he, unless there were full life after death and unless the righteous enjoyed a destiny different from that of the wicked?

This meandering explanation is more than an academic exercise in Old Testament backgrounds. It is precisely what we need if we want to understand what Jesus and his apostles teach us about heaven and hell. Those great biblical realities became clear only when the Savior came to rescue us from the one and point us to the other.

The New Testament mentions heaven and hell, and with considerable frequency. Yet both those abodes of the dead defy adequate description. Perhaps God has purposely left most of the details about them draped in mystery. It is more important for us to know the *why* of heaven and hell than the *what*. It is good for us to know what heaven and hell are *for*, even though we may not grasp what they are *like*. Hell is for separation; heaven is for fellowship. Those statements do not tell us all, but they do tell us what counts most.

Hell Is for Separation

Jesus' pictorial description of life after death reminds us that hell is for separation. The rich man plagued with torment "saw Abraham far off and Lazarus in his bosom" (Lk 16:23). When the rich man begged for relief from thirst, Abraham described the vast separation between the righteous and the wicked: "Between us and you a great chasm has been fixed, in order that those who would pass from here to you may not be able, and none may cross from there to us" (Lk 16:26).

Separated from Abraham and the rest of the righteous, the rich man was also cut off from access to his living loved ones. He could not send even the most urgent message to his five brothers to warn them of the peril of hell (Lk 16:27-31). And he was separated from God. His thirst, his torment, his distance from Abraham, his frustration at his inability to communicate with his family all suggest that. The grace and goodness that had sustained and blessed him in life were withdrawn. Hell is the only adequate name for such separation.

The separation is tragic because it is avoidable. In the case of the rich man in Jesus' story, a compassionate treatment of the servant Lazarus would have made the difference. For all of us, repentance and faith mark the difference between heaven and hell. To turn from our self-sufficiency and rebellion and to trust God for forgiveness and new life are what God asks of us. What makes hell hell, in part at least, must be the realization that it was avoidable, that a positive response to God's grace would have made all the difference. Perhaps this burning, gnawing sense of tragedy accounts for Jesus' description of hell as a place "where their worm does not die, and the fire is not quenched" (Mk 9:48).

The separation is painful because it is inhuman. The images of torment—thirst and fire—are ways of highlighting the inhumanity of hell. But, at root, hell is inhuman because it is godless. What is human life but life lived in dependence on and fellowship with God? Any other life is not life at all, but anguish-laden death. The physical horrors of hell are graphic ways of hinting at the real pain—absence of God's good presence, an absence which dooms life to degradation and destruction.

As tragic and as painful as the separation is, its worst feature is that the separation is irreversible. Not one hint did Jesus give in his story that the rich man would have another chance if he could endure the torment for a while. History moves on and does not turn back. It gives me opportunity during the years of my accountability to make my decision to go God's way and be his person. If I fail to use that opportunity, life rolls on without me. Death and hell become my lot.

I once stood sleepily in the terminal at a small Idaho airport, waiting for the attendant to come and check my suitcase. The roar of the propellers stabbed me awake. I dashed out to the edge of the runway in time to see my plane taxiing for takeoff. I blurted out my panic to the attendant, who rushed inside to radio the pilot. The plane returned, lowered its stairway and clutched me aboard, bag in hand. I rejoiced in my second chance. History, however, will not give that opportunity. Hell is full of people who know better now. We cannot wait to do God's will.

Hell is for separation. And that separation is irreversible, painful and tragic.

Heaven Is for Fellowship

Heaven is the place where the life of the living God is experienced in its fullness. Its most beautiful and most persistent characteristic is fellowship. It is the state in which we are with God without the hindrance of any distraction or imperfection.

The fellowship is immediate. For the man or woman, boy or girl, who trusts Jesus as Lord and Savior, there is no gap between death and heaven: "Today you will be with me in Paradise," Jesus promised the thief crucified at his side (Lk 23:43). "Away from the body and at home with the Lord" was Paul's definition of Christian death (2 Cor 5:8). Life is life with the living God, and there can be no intermission, no blank space. We live with God on earth sustained by his presence. That life continues unbroken in our transfer from earth to heaven, where we wait for the Second Coming of Christ, the resurrection of the body, and the new heavens and new earth.

The fellowship is transforming, just as it is immediate. Life in heaven not only continues our life with God; it makes it better. Remember Paul's exclamation: "For to me to live is Christ, and to die is gain" (Phil 1:21). All fellowship with God on earth takes place in clouded circumstances; we cannot bask in the fullness of his love because the things of the world get in the way. All earthly tables are prepared for us in the presence of enemies. Sin, suffering and persecution together with the world, the flesh and the devil are ever present to keep us from being all that we were meant to be. None of them has a passport valid in heaven; they are all halted at the gates. That means that all the beautiful human characteristics that God wants to nurture within us will be nurtured without opposition or competition. Heaven is for fellowship with God, and that fellowship will work even greater wonders in heaven than it has on earth. Think how far God has already brought you, and then rejoice ahead of time for what is yet to happen.

The fellowship is permanent. God has surprises for his people even beyond heaven, as we shall see in our study of the new heavens and earth. But of one thing we can be sure: once we join him in heaven, we can never be separated from him again. His life will sustain us eternally. He is through all eternity the living God, and he has called us to live at his side, continually renewed and refreshed by his life. What a hope! By his side forever. What a sight! His face before us for all eternity.

No pyramids or vast memorials are necessary. The living God is with us and for us. He has spoken his words of life in the Bible. We want to keep hearing them and trusting them. They are a more powerful witness to the realities of heaven and hell than the appearance of a person back from the dead. The rich man's concern for himself and his five brothers was too late. We must repent and believe while the opportunity is before us. God's Word tolerates no trifling in matters so vital to human life and human death.

Then if any one says to you, "Lo, here is the Christ!" or "There he is!" do not believe it. For false Christs and false prophets will arise and show great signs and wonders, so as to lead astray, if possible, even the elect. Lo, I have told you beforehand. So, if they say to you, "Lo, he is in the wilderness," do not go out; if they say, "Lo, he is in the inner rooms," do not believe it. For as the lightning comes from the east and shines as far as the west, so will be the coming of the Son of man. Wherever the body is, there the eagles will be gathered together.

Immediately after the tribulation of those days the sun will be darkened, and the moon will not give its light, and the stars will fall from heaven, and the powers of the heavens will be shaken; then will appear the sign of the Son of man in heaven, and then all the tribes of the earth will mourn, and they will see the Son of man coming on the clouds of heaven with power and great glory; and he will send out his angels with a loud trumpet call, and they will gather his elect from the four winds, from one end of heaven to the other.

Matthew 24:23-31

5

The Glorious Coming

IT WOULD BE HARD to think of a sharper contrast. Christ's second coming will be so different from his first that the contrast is almost incredible.

Think what the Jews and Romans who watched the crucifixion must have thought of him. He was a condemned man, forsaken by his closest friends and unwilling to defend himself. His companions in crucifixion were notorious thieves. Possessions he had none; even his cloak was stripped from him at the end. Body bloodied from the lash, brow punctured by thorns, side gouged with the spear, frame wrenched out of joint from his weight pulling against the nails—he was a picture of disgrace and humiliation.

Those who watched that ignominious defeat could have had no idea of Christ's power and glory. They might have pitied but they could not have honored him. They might have acknowledged his courage in the face of suffering, but they could not have recognized his deity. They might have been pained by his anguish, but they would not have looked to him for salvation.

By and large that has been the reaction of the world to Jesus ever since. It has gone its way, assuming that Jesus was at most a heroic martyr, but it has not worshiped him as God in the flesh and Lord over history. Too much shame, too much defeat, too much agony hovered over his last days to encourage faith, let alone worship.

Can the kingdom of God be present in such menial and miserable circumstances? That was the question at the time and has been ever since. The Incarnation was a mystery which only the faithful could understand, those to whom God had revealed the truth of his presence in Christ. "God was in Christ." That is a central declaration of the Christian faith, but its truth is by no means obvious to the world.

But one day it will be. That is what Christ promised when he spoke of his second coming: "Then will appear the sign of the Son of man in heaven, and then all the tribes of the earth will mourn, and they will see the Son of man coming on the clouds of heaven with power and great glory; and he will send out his angels . . . and they will gather his elect from the four winds" (Mt 24:30-31). What a contrast to the crucifixion!

Public in Its Display

By and large the birth of Jesus went unnoticed by the world around Palestine. The shepherds heard the angels and told their friends and neighbors. Wise men followed the star, conversed with Herod and returned to their land, probably to have their story fall on skeptical ears. No trembling was felt on the Tiber where Augustus Caesar ruled his far-flung empire. No terror gripped the hearts of scholars in Alexandria and Athens where the ancient universities carried on their work. No Persian general mobilized troops to respond to a military threat. Neither politics, scholarship nor warfare was much affected by Mary's little baby.

Yet he was God visiting our planet, planning to defeat the hosts of Satan, destined to sit on David's throne, offering forgiveness to the human family. Though Herod worried about his birth and Pilate refused to stop his execution, what Jesus left behind him posed no menace to the political structures of Palestine—at least no menace that they understood. A handful of ardent disciples and a hundred or so other followers—what could they do to influence the course of world history?

The Second Coming is to be different. It will be public in its brilliant display of Christ's power and glory. It will reveal to the entire world what the church has already learned from Christ's apostles: Jesus is the Son of God, the Lord, the Savior.

The metaphors used by Jesus highlight this public aspect of his return: "For as the lightning comes from the east and shines as far as the west, so will be the coming of the Son of man. Wherever the body is, there the eagles [or vultures] will be gathered together" (Mt 24:27-28). Jesus' point is plain. There will be no secrets about his second coming. Rumors of false messiahs can be dismissed with a wave of the hand. Anyone who comes without the public display that flashes across the heavens like lightning is not the returning Christ. Anyone who does not attract full public attention to himself, as a carcass lures vultures by the score, is not the Savior come again.

The terms in the New Testament also underscore the public nature of the Second Coming. Christ's coming is described as an "arrival" (*parousia* in 1 Thess 3:13; 4:15; 2 Thess 2:8). The word was often used of the coming of a great military or political leader. It suggests pomp and ceremony, prancing steeds and cheering throngs, banners unfurled to the tattoo of drums. So with Jesus: trumpets will blast, archangels will shout, clouds will descend. His coming is an arrival, full of power and glory.

It is also described as a "revelation" (*apokalypsis* in 1 Cor 1:7; 2 Thess 1:6-7; 1 Pet 4:13), an unveiling. What can this mean but that all the mystery, all the hiddenness we now experience when we ponder Christ's glory, will be done away with? We shall see him as he is, the Son of God in whom all God's fullness dwells. History's dark side will be made bright. God's purposes will come truly clear. Christ's coming is a revelation, resplendent with power and glory.

The biblical writers use a third term, "manifestation" (*epiphaneia* in 2 Thess 2:8; 1 Tim 6:14; 2 Tim 4:8), to depict the brightness, the visual splendor of the Second Coming. It is this manifestation, this epiphany, that we as Christians are to love and long for (2 Tim 4:8). It is this manifestation that Paul calls "our blessed hope" (Tit 2:13). Christ will show himself as King and Conqueror to his people and the world. Christ's coming is a manifestation, brilliant with power and glory.

Cosmic in Its Impact

Christ's second coming is a public event, shouting its message of lordship and kingdom around the world. It is also an event cosmic in its total impact. The universe itself will participate in it: "Immediately after the tribulation of those days the sun will be darkened, and the moon will not give its light, and the stars will fall from heaven, and the powers of the heavens will be shaken; then will appear the sign of the Son of man in heaven" (Mt 24:29-30).

God is on the move, and the whole universe bows in awe before him. The glory of his presence is so bright that it pales the sun and moon and blanks out the stars and the constellations (here called "the powers of the heavens"). The language is like Isaiah's poetry:

Then the moon will be confounded,
and the sun ashamed;
for the LORD of hosts will reign
on Mount Zion and in Jerusalem
and before his elders he will manifest his glory.
(Is 24:23)

The picture of a confounded moon and a shame-stricken sun is especially impressive when we remember that most of Israel's neighbors worshiped the moon and the sun. Yet, says the prophet, they cannot compare in brilliance to the presence of God when he establishes his kingdom.

Redemption is on the way, and the whole universe longs to share in it. Our sin is so horrible in its impact that the whole universe is affected by it. Thorns grew up as obstacles to work. Serpents became enemies of human beings. The creation seemed to be at odds with itself. It proclaims the glory of God, while it groans like a mother in labor for God's final victory (Rom 8:19-23). What does Christ's coming mean but that redemption is on the way? The new heaven and the new earth where all is right with God are just around the corner. The darkened sun and moon, the erased stars and planets, are the final groanings before that great day of redemption when everything in the universe will be as God would want it.

Divisive in Its Effect

If Jesus' return will have such a startling impact on the universe, what will it do to the people of the world? Jesus' answer to that question was blunt, even stark: "Then all the tribes of the earth will mourn, and they will see the Son of man coming on the clouds of heaven with power and great glory; and he will send out his angels with a loud trumpet call, and they will gather his elect from the four winds, from one end of heaven to the other" (Mt 24:30-31).

History is heading toward the great divide. Christ's second coming means unification, yes; but it also means division. Christ and all his elect will be united; the universe itself will run more harmoniously than at any time since creation. Yet the tribes of earth will mourn.

The tribes of the earth will mourn as they realize the wrongness of their ways. They practiced religions that are proved false by Christ's return. They followed moral standards which are exposed as bankrupt. They had a view of history that was inadequate. In fact, most of them had thought that history would never end. Now, in mourning, they watch it come to a conclusion which condemns them. Above all, Jesus' return exposes their foolish views of him. They did not believe his claim to be God's Son; they did not accept his offer of salvation; they did not bow before his lordship.

Now all they can do is mourn—mourn the wrongness of their ways, and mourn the sternness of his judgment. Their fate in choosing wrongly is not just embarrassment; it is punishment. All the power and glory of the Second Coming leave them not hopeful but condemned. Christ's coming is divisive in its ultimate effect.

The elect will be gathered by the angels. That is the other side of the division. God's people—Jews and Gentiles—who have clung to Christ's saving them will be united with each other and their Lord and Savior. No place will be too remote for the angels to reach; no language will be too foreign for them to speak; no believer will be too insignificant for them to gather. Christ's power and glory will thrill them with expectation. The great reunion of God's family which they waited for daily will finally have come.

That great day (and may it come quickly!) will startle the world with its message. Like a cosmic bulletin board, the heavens will shout the words of victory. We need to hear and believe that shout ahead of time.

Jesus' return is a shout of vindication. It will convince the world beyond doubt that Bethlehem's baby, the Nazarene carpenter, is indeed God in the flesh. What was hidden in the past will be fully evident. The incognito Son of God will strip the veil away and show himself for what he is. And no one, *no one*, will argue to the contrary.

Jesus' return is a shout of salvation. It announces to the world and to angels that what human ingenuity could not accomplish divine power has achieved. All that God wanted to happen when he spoke creation into life and breathed his breath into our human frame will be done. And by him! The universe itself will join the party and rejoice in the will of God. The whole creation will lift in unison its exclamation: Salvation belongs to the Lord!

Jesus' return, however, is also a shout of judgment. It will divide the world into those who have truly believed and those who have not. It will make permanent the decisions of faith and nonfaith made by the entire human family.

We need to hear this shout beforehand, even as we will hear it at the end—the shout of vindication, of salvation, of judgment. And we need to shout our response right now. Lord, I believe! Jesus is Lord! Even so, come quickly!

Then I saw thrones, and seated on them were those to whom judgment was committed. Also I saw the souls of those who had been beheaded for their testimony to Jesus and for the word of God, and who had not worshiped the beast or its image and had not received its mark on their foreheads or their hands. They came to life, and reigned with Christ a thousand years. The rest of the dead did not come to life until the thousand years were ended. This is the first resurrection. Blessed and holy is he who shares in the first resurrection! Over such the second death has no power, but they shall be priests of God and of Christ, and they shall reign with him a thousand years.
Revelation 20:4-6

6
The
First
Resurrection

WHERE IS THE church headed?

That question has popped to the surface in a hundred different forms. It is a favorite of newspeople and television interviewers. They wonder where the tides of history will lead God's people—tides that seem so contrary. The tides of secularism and immorality seem to be engulfing whole sectors of the Western world, just at the time that currents of Christian vitality appear stronger than at any time in the past half century. In the Marxist world, which seems to enlarge in scope and influence year by year, worship of God and instruction in the faith go on under almost strangling restrictions, yet reports from China and Iron Curtain countries tell of full churches and dedicated congregations.

Where is the church headed? The worldwide journeys of Pope John Paul II and his strong pronouncements have raised that question on the cover of national magazines and in the religion columns of prominent newspapers. Can the Pope rally the divided camps within Catholicism so that the forces of communism, secularism, paganism and modernism can be adequately resisted? Will he be open to closer contacts with various Protestant and Eastern Orthodox churches, so that gaps can be closed and divisions repaired among Christians worldwide?

It is not an idle question. Where the church is headed has a significance beyond what most of those asking or answering it realize. Where the church is headed is a much more important matter than, say, how far we should let inflation go before we check it, or how long our energy supply will last. Where the church is headed is an issue that lies at the heart of human history. It is no less a question than this: What will be the outcome of God's work in history?

The question is too important to be left to religious scholars, news analysts or Christian ministers. Humanly speaking, the evidence is too ambiguous to allow any utterly reliable answer. The answers tend to come out in the hedging formula, "On the one hand, ... but then on the other ..."

Fortunately we have solid news of where the church is headed that takes us beyond the ambiguity of worldly evidence and human opinion. We have God-given photos of the church's future that answer unequivocally the crucial question. The book of Revelation shouts the answer: The church is headed for rewards and reunion. When? At the first resurrection, when Jesus returns to establish his millennial reign.

Few passages in the Bible tell us more about the church's future than the brief paragraph in Revelation 20:4-6. It addresses with power, clarity and finality three of the most persistent questions plaguing the human family. Those questions need some pursuing.

Where the Real Power Lies

The question of power is central to all discussions of why history goes as it does. Estimates of power are made in various ways: the size of fleets, number of battle-ready divisions, stockpiles of nuclear weapons, size of military budget. These are all factors by which some analysts weigh power, power to defend against attack, power to aid allies, power to back up political bargaining.

Economic wealth is another measurement of power. A stable currency, a favorable balance of trade, a growing volume in gross national product, an ability to deal with indebtedness—these are some of the financial indicators that add up to economic health.

Political prowess is still another component of power as we usually define it. Nations that have skilled diplomats and seasoned negotiators, nations whose word is trustworthy and whose promises are kept, nations whose motives are above-board and whose humanitarian concerns are respected—these are the political entities that are held in repute as influential in the court of world affairs.

As important as these military, economic and political expressions of power may be, however, they do not give the best or highest answer to the question of where the power lies. That answer comes to us from John's vision of the future as recorded in the book of Revelation: "Then I saw thrones, and seated on them were those to whom judgment was committed" (Rev 20:4).

The language rings with power: thrones, persons seated on them, judgment committed to them. It is a powerful, indeed a regal, scene. A couple of questions flow out of it. First, what is meant by the *judgment*? The best definition is found in the words that immediately follow: "They came to life, and reigned with Christ a thousand years" (v. 4); and again, "but they shall be priests of God and of Christ, and they shall reign with him a thousand years" (v. 6). The biblical idea of judgment can include the idea of ruling or reigning, not just the notion of making decisions in court. The Old Testament judges, for instance, were not magistrates who decided the law so much as governors who led the people.

"Judgment" then is a description of the ruling authority which those who sit on the throne will share with Jesus Christ. That conclusion, in turn, prompts another question: Who are those who sit on the throne and exercise judgment by reigning with Christ? The passage itself does not directly answer the question, though it does say that "they came to life," that is, they were raised from the dead (v. 4).

From Paul's description of Christ's coming in 1 Thessalonians 4, we know that it is Christian believers who are raised from the dead to join Christ in the air. Probably, then, those who sit on the thrones are the Christians, those who trusted Jesus as Lord and Savior and were raised to meet him at his coming.

The Bible is consistent and insistent in teaching that Christ's power to reign will be shared with all believers. Here are Jesus' words on the matter: "Truly, I say to you, in the new world, when the Son of man shall sit on his glorious throne, you who have followed me will also sit on twelve thrones, judging the twelve tribes of Israel" (Mt 19:28). Paul expands that idea to include the world: "Do you not know that the saints will judge the world?" (1 Cor 6:2). The Revelation echoes this promise of ruling power by promising a share in Jesus' throne to all who are overcomers (Rev 2:26; 3:21).

Part of the reward, in other words, for truly serving Jesus is to share in his power and authority as he sets up his earthly reign. Think of what this meant to a church nearly stifled in the smoke of Roman persecution, tempted to cower before the power of Caesar's throne. Not there by the banks of the Tiber, not there in the legions of Rome, not there in the coffers rich with imperial taxes does the power lie. Jesus is Lord. And those who are part of his body will share, in public and powerful display, the fullness of that lordship.

Who the True Victors Are

While there are many definitions of winning, one thing is common to most of them: the fact of survival. It would be hard for a football team to win if all the members were carted to the infirmary before the game was over. It would be difficult for a country to claim victory in a battle where all its troops were destroyed. It would be impossible for a company to claim triumph in a business competition which drove it into bankruptcy.

In most of our human definitions, victory includes survival. But the Bible knows better. It often grants victory to those who seem thoroughly crushed, viciously destroyed. In our scene in the Revelation, the victors are those who were savagely beheaded: "I saw the souls of those who had been beheaded for their testimony to Jesus and for the word of God, and who had not worshiped the beast or its image and had not received its mark on their foreheads or their hands" (Rev 20:4).

Who are the true victors? To answer this question the camera of Revelation zooms in on a particular group within the church. To the whole church is given authority to rule. The resurrected, believing Christians sit on the thrones. The camera pans the entire scene and then focuses sharply on part of that vast company, the Christians martyred by the powers of the antichrist, called here by his suitable title, the beast.

These victors, especially saluted, are not those who survived but those who died. Everything about them seemed to suggest defeat to those who had known them. They had been crushed by a powerful government, ground down by a cruel dictator, done in by brutal executioners. Their reputations had been tarred and their properties confiscated. The last thing that anyone would have called them was conquerors. Yet they are pictured as alive from the dead, as priests of God, as co-rulers with Christ.

What made them victorious? Jesus' lordship had called for their full obedience. His word had summoned them to true loyalty. And they had said yes. At the same time, they had disobeyed the rules of antichrist's government in obedience to the higher rules of Jesus' reign. By saying yes to Christ and no to antichrist, they had demonstrated their own loyalty and their own obedience and were equipped to help Jesus rule for the millennium of power and righteousness which was part of his program.

What the Final Outcome Is

Where is the church headed? Toward the first resurrection with its reunion with Christ and its rewards of power, glory and fellowship. That is history's final outcome for all who truly learn history's meaning.

The hindrances to wholeness of life have been put aside. *Death is defeated.* Christ's coming has brought in its wake resurrection for those who have loved him. "The rest of the dead did not come to life until the thousand years were ended. This is the first resurrection. Blessed and holy is he who shares in the first resurrection!" (Rev 20:5-6). Physical death, which will hold unbelievers in its clutches until the final resurrection with its judgment, has had its grip broken by Jesus' resurrection and by his second coming. Believers are reunited with their bodies, with their Christian loved ones and with their Christ. But, even more, spiritual death is defeated. No damning judgment, no terrifying separation will be their lot. Life and victory await them, and for ever: "Over such the second death has no power, but they shall be priests of God and of Christ" (v. 6).

Death is defeated and *fellowship is assured.* That is the meaning of our eternal priesthood—constant access to God. We pray to him, worship him, serve him and his people, not from a distance but before his face. That is the ultimate reward, the most joyful part of the last chapter of history's story, the unending chapter. We stand face-to-face with God for eternity. Think of the glory; think of the wonder; think of the love. All that God has shown himself to be in the Bible, in Jesus and in the Holy Spirit, we shall see and know for ourselves in his presence.

Let the commentators and reporters speculate. Let the church's fans and critics ply their theories. You and I can smile, believe and rejoice as those who know for certain the answer as to where the church is headed. It is headed for resurrection that conquers death; it is headed for fellowship that tolerates no separation.

The question is not about the church. Its destiny is settled. The question is about us. Will we be part of that church through faith in its living Lord?

Lest you be wise in your own conceits, I want you to understand this mystery, brethren: a hardening has come upon part of Israel, until the full number of the Gentiles come in, and so all Israel will be saved; as it is written,

"The Deliverer will come from Zion,
he will banish ungodliness from Jacob";
"and this will be my covenant with them
when I take away their sins."

As regards the gospel they are enemies of God, for your sake; but as regards election they are beloved for the sake of their forefathers. For the gifts and the call of God are irrevocable. Just as you were once disobedient to God but now have received mercy because of their disobedience, so they have now been disobedient in order that by the mercy shown to you they also may receive mercy. For God has consigned all men to disobedience, that he may have mercy upon all.

Romans 11:25-32

7

The Future of Israel

ISRAEL SEEMS TO be in the headlines with relentless regularity. The prolonged struggles in Lebanon, the cycles of terrorist raids and Israeli retaliation, the negotiations over the West Bank of the Jordan or a permanent home for the Palestinians, the arguments and counterarguments about the Old City, the purchase of military equipment by one side or the other—these and a score of other items conspire to grab an inordinate amount of newspaper space and television time.

Why the publicity for Israel? Its population is not large, about like that of one of our smaller states or larger cities. Its terrain is not extensive, not much larger than Egypt's delta area. You could plant the whole territory of Israel in a corner of Saudi Arabia and scarcely notice it.

Why the headlines for Israel? One obvious reason is the suffering the Jews have undergone in the past generation. And when, having survived one of history's most vicious and sweeping death plots, they went on to form a new nation and to reclaim old land, they did so with the good will of much of the Western world.

A second reason for our awareness of Israel is the geographical importance of its land. Palestine, as we used to call the territory that Israel reclaimed, has been a central plot of ground in world history for millenniums. It formed a bridge between Egypt and Mesopotamia across which the soldiers and merchants of the two great valleys marched from the beginnings of civilization. Whichever valley controlled Palestine was in a position to dominate the other valley, whether the Nile wanted to lord it over the Tigris-Euphrates or the other way around. Add to this geographical picture the presence of oil, found in unmeasured abundance in the Arab world, and we can begin to understand the headlines.

Israel's prominence can also be explained by the presence of Jews in so many European and North and South American countries. Most of them have never visited Tel Aviv or Jerusalem; many of them have roots generations deep in the countries where they live and carry citizenship. Some of them have lost touch with their Jewish faith. But virtually all of them are concerned with Israel's welfare. Just as they identified with the horrors of the holocaust, even though their immediate families may not have been affected, so they identify with Israel's woes or welfare now. They read the headlines eager for every word of peace.

We may have to dig even more deeply for the full explanation of the attention accorded Israel, however. History, geography and ethnic attachment account for much but not for all of the priority given to the tiny, feisty nation. The deepest reasons may be spiritual. Both the land of Israel and the Hebrew people have been central to God's program from Abraham's time forward. To them God revealed his love and power. To them he gave his commandments and promises. To them he sent his only Son. Their place in God's program means that, as long as history lasts, they will have a prominence beyond their size and numbers.

And the future headlines will outshout the past. Israel's ups and downs may continue for a while —perhaps a long while. But the ultimate destiny is up, not down. On that we have God's word.

One of the great features of Christ's second coming is what it will mean to the Jews of the world. It will answer their hopes and fulfill their destiny as surely as it does for the Christian church. The people of God, whom he chose four thousand years ago, will one day be saved. That is Scripture's firm promise.

To understand, we have to see the three stages through which God has worked out (and will yet work out) his choice of the people who love and serve him. With help from Paul's letter to the Romans, we shall look at God's work of election (or choosing) as it has unfolded through the course of history. We cannot know what Jesus' second coming will be like without this perspective.

The Choice Extended
The story begins with God's command to Abraham, a command that was followed by God's promise: "Go from your country and your kindred and your father's house to the land that I will show you. And I will make of you a great nation, and I will bless you, and make your name great, so that you will be a blessing. I will bless those who bless you, and him who curses you I will curse; and by you all the families of the earth shall bless themselves" (Gen 12:1-3).

God himself extended the choice. He selected Abraham and sealed that selection with magnificent promises. We have no clues about Abraham's previous spiritual condition. Was he seeking God? Was he an extraordinarily righteous man? We are not told. The spotlight is not on Abraham but on God. He has the authority to command and the power to promise. He chose Abraham before Abraham chose him.

God extended the choice for the sake of all nations. Though Abraham has center stage, it is not he alone who is the subject of the promises. Beyond Abraham are all the families of the earth who will find blessing through his name. One family was snatched by God from homeland and kindred in order that a multitude of families would come to know that living God. Forty centuries ago God spoke to a man in Haran north of the bend of the Euphrates, and, as he did, God had you and me in mind in Denver, Calgary, London and Rio de Janeiro. God chose Abraham not just for Abraham's sake but for ours. His people were to be a light to the nations, and we have been led out of darkness by their light.

Abraham responded to God's choice with faith and obedience. Genesis is succinct: "So Abram went, as the LORD had told him; and Lot went with him" (Gen 12:4). A little later in the story we read, "And [Abram] believed the LORD; and he reckoned it to him as righteousness" (15:6).

Abram went; Abram believed. His response to the command and the promises modeled the way of faith for all of God's people. Those who would truly belong to him go when he commands, come if he calls, and believe what he promises. Abraham has become the spiritual example (the father, if you will) to all who would heed God's call. Neither ceremony, ritual nor law was his response, but faith and obedience. Thus was God's choice extended and accepted. To use Paul's image, the olive tree was planted. Its roots, trunk and branches were to grow to mighty proportions.

The Choice Expanded

The second stage of God's program was triggered by another command and another promise—this time to Saul of Tarsus, a descendant of Abraham. He was met by Christ on the road to Damascus and ordered to enter the city to receive his commands (Acts 22:8-10). The command was "to serve and bear witness to the things in which you have seen me [Jesus] and to those in which I will appear to you" (Acts 26:16). The promise was an assurance of protection: "[I am] delivering you from the people and from the Gentiles—to whom I send you to open their eyes, that they may turn from darkness to light and from the power of Satan to God, that they may receive forgiveness of sins and a place among those who are sanctified by faith in me" (Acts 26:17-18).

The light, the faith, the hope, the promise, the forgiveness offered to Abraham and his family were now being extended beyond them—far beyond them—to the nations of the world. The pledge that God made to Abraham was rushing toward fulfillment: the nations were going to be blessed through the life and faith of Abraham as Paul proclaimed it. An abundant harvest of Gentiles was to be reaped. Sons and daughters from every continent were to be chosen for the family of God. The light that had blinded Saul on the road to Damascus was to blaze through the darkness in almost every nation of the planet.

And what about the people of Israel? A loyal remnant of Jews would remain, men and women whose hearts were open to the Spirit and grace of God. In almost every synagogue where Paul (as Saul of Tarsus was renamed) journeyed, some Jewish people confessed their faith in Jesus as Messiah and were baptized into his church.

But the vast majority of Jews rejected the message of Jesus' followers and persisted in their efforts to gain God's favor by works of law. *Harden-*

ing is the term that Paul used in Romans 11:25 to describe what had happened. It is a strong term, one which would have stung the Jews who heard it. "Hardening" is what had happened to Pharaoh in Moses' day. He had hardened his heart—set his will—so consistently and determinedly against God that God finally let him have his way by making it impossible for him to change his mind (Ex 8:32; 10:1). Now, Paul was saying, something of what Pharaoh, the most hated enemy of Israel, had experienced would happen to the Israelites themselves.

The choice that began with Abraham was now expanded as the gospel was carried to the Gentiles. Again Paul used the figure of the olive tree: "But if some of the branches [some of the Jews] were broken off, and you, a wild olive shoot [Gentiles in Rome], were grafted in their place to share the richness of the olive tree, do not boast over the branches. If you do boast, remember it is not you that support the root, but the root that supports you. . . . They were broken off because of their unbelief, but you stand fast only through faith. So do not become proud, but stand in awe" (Rom 11:17-20).

Faith in God's grace is the key to life. Neither Jew nor Gentile dares boast of station, race or calling. Awe before the mystery of God's ways is the only proper attitude. Jewish branches have been pruned; Gentile branches have been grafted. But the whole tree from Abraham's trunk to the latest sprout is God's doing. He extended the choice in the first place; he expanded it to include people from all nations in the second.

The Choice Reissued

God will issue the choice again, in a third stage, to the Jewish people when his time comes: "For if you [Gentiles] have been cut from what is by nature a wild olive tree, and grafted, contrary to nature, into a cultivated olive tree [God's program among Israel], how much more will these natural branches [the Jews] be grafted back into their own olive tree" (Rom 11:24).

The greatest headlines featuring Israel are yet to be made. The most dramatic chapter in God's dealing with them is yet to come. It is clearly promised in Scripture. Israel's hardening, unlike Pharaoh's, will not be permanent. "I want you to understand this mystery, brethren: a hardening has come upon part of Israel, until the full number of the Gentiles come in, and so all Israel will be saved" (Rom 11:25-26).

What will bring that about? Paul does not give the full answer, but he does hint at one possibility: the jealousy of the Jews (Rom 11:13-14). Their feelings that they have been crowded from the center of God's program may encourage them to be open to God's grace and to seek his full acceptance in Christ. This will happen most fully and finally at Christ's second coming. The revelation of his power and glory will lead his ancient people to look to him as Messiah and Savior:

The Deliverer will come from Zion,
he will banish ungodliness from Jacob. (Rom 11:26)

Paul's confession to Jesus as Messiah (like the confession of any Jew since) is a foretaste of that great day.

Paul's words about the Jews are a warning against all forms of anti-Semitism. God will continue to care for his chosen people and will lead many back to him at the end. Jew-baiting, Jew-hating, Jew-rejecting Christians stand under dire threat of judgment. Paul's words are an invitation to faithful witness to Jewish people. He himself longed for their salvation. We need lovingly and winsomely to recognize our spiritual ties to them, even as we witness to our faith in Jesus who is the Christ.

Paul's final word was a doxology to God, who can work such wonders. The God who can by grace save both Jews and Gentiles, the God whose brightest headlines are yet to be read, the God who can plant a trunk, prune off branches, graft in new branches, and then regraft old branches is a God before whose mysteries we lift our hearts in praise:

"O the depth of the riches and wisdom and knowledge of God! How unsearchable are his judgments and how inscrutable his ways!" (Rom 11:33).

Then I saw an angel coming down from heaven, holding in his hand the key of the bottomless pit and a great chain. And he seized the dragon, that ancient serpent, who is the Devil and Satan, and bound him for a thousand years, and threw him into the pit, and shut it and sealed it over him, that he should deceive the nations no more, till the thousand years were ended. After that he must be loosed for a little while. . . .

And when the thousand years are ended, Satan will be loosed from his prison and will come out to deceive the nations which are at the four corners of the earth, that is, Gog and Magog, to gather then for battle; their number is like the sand of the sea. And they marched up over the broad earth and surrounded the camp of the saints and the beloved city; but fire came down from heaven and consumed them, and the devil who had deceived them was thrown into the lake of fire and sulphur where the beast and the false prophet were, and they will be tormented day and night for ever and ever.

Revelation 20:1-3, 7-10

8

The Triumphal Millennium

SOME QUESTIONS can be answered only by revelation. Our normal means of investigation are not sufficient. We cannot solve them by mathematics, microscope or telescope. They will not yield to the tools of the scientist's laboratory or to the books in the philosopher's study. Because they are questions that pertain to God, they defy all our human ingenuity. We will have no answers to them, unless God gives them to us.

These unsolvable questions are not trivial; they touch the most basic issues of our living. They are not refinements to what we already know, decorating our knowledge as pictures do our walls. They are fundamental to our well-being, like the foundations on which our houses are built.

Which questions are of this sort? These, for a start: What is God like? What does God expect of me? How can I be right with God? Unless we hear from God on these, they go unanswered and, further, they remain unanswerable. We can guess at them, as the religions of the world have done, but we can give them no sure response.

To answer them was one reason that Jesus came the first time. In his holiness, love, wisdom and power we see the fullness of God. Never again does the human family have to guess about God's nature. "God is like Jesus" is the answer shouted to us from the pages of New Testament history.

In Jesus' commands to his disciples we hear God's eager expectations of us—trust in and worship of him, love and service to one another. And in Jesus' death and resurrection the ground is laid for us to be right with God. Forgiveness for our failings and reconciliation for our estrangement are the great gifts that those events make possible. But these answers were not blazed on the sky in heavenly neon; they were not trumpeted from the mountaintop with stereophonic speakers. They were lived out in the words and deeds of Jesus, who came to dwell among us.

Yet some questions remain, questions which likewise can be answered only by revelation. Will evil win in the end? What is righteousness really like? Is judgment truly fair? These questions continue to nag us as we leaf through history's pages and watch the nightly news.

To answer them is one of the reasons for Christ's second coming. History has raised the questions, and they can best be answered within that history. As Christians we believe that Christ's second coming is not just an idea, symbol or picture. Biblical descriptions of it are not just poems or parables about God's mythical victories. The Second Coming will be an event within history. When it happens we will be able to mark its date on a calendar; we will be able to trace its impact on a map.

Satan fights God's people in actual historical experience—through daily temptation and through corrupt organizations, whether businesses, governments, churches, unions or crime syndicates. Righteousness, if it is to mean anything, has to be lived out in history. God's will is already done in heaven. It is this earth of ours that is the problem —this earth with its crooked politicians, selfish parents, rebellious children, cheating merchants, immoral preachers, corruptible police, oppressive bosses and lazy employees. Judgment, to be fair, has to take into consideration the opportunities we have had in daily life to see righteousness at work and to repent of our wicked ways.

For all these reasons and more, Christ will come into our history once again. And by that coming he will answer another set of questions which only he can answer. He will answer them not in secret conferences with church leaders but before the eyes and ears of the world. His coming does not close history; it opens history's last chapter—a period of glory and splendor, of revelation and vindication, slated to last a thousand years. The millennium, as we call that period, is history's last great classroom in which Christ himself will be the Teacher and his curriculum will be life's perennial questions. We will look at three of them.

Will Evil Win in the End?

The power of evil seems overwhelming. Wicked governments seem on the increase and attempts to rule righteously and humanely seem to be scoffed at. Stories of crime, persecution and tragedy hog the news, and we have to read the paper's back pages to catch the tidbits of good news.

Will evil win? Because of evil's seeming power in our world, this is not an idle question. Its answer determines whether history will finally prove worthwhile.

The millennium helps to answer the question with a ringing *no!* It marks one of the great stages in Christ's victory over Satan. Consider this graphic description of the scene: "Then I saw an angel coming down from heaven, holding in his hand the key of the bottomless pit and a great chain. And he seized the dragon, that ancient serpent, who is the Devil and Satan, and bound him for a thousand years, and threw him into the pit, and shut it and sealed it over him, that he should deceive the nations no more, till the thousand years were ended. After that he must be loosed for a little while" (Rev 20:1-3).

We see here a monumental battle in the age-long war between God and Satan. The war began in the Garden of Eden when Satan seemed to defeat Adam and Eve, and yet himself was cursed by

God's word and frustrated in his plan by God's grace, which preserved the first couple and enabled them to raise up the line of Seth to love and worship God. The war continued in the story of Job, where Satan was again defeated by Job's faith in the midst of suffering. The battle blazed brightly when Jesus demonstrated God's sovereign rule by casting out demons and overturning their mastery of human life. Not only that, but Jesus decisively smashed Satan's attack on him by thwarting the triple temptation through the power of the Scriptures. Then in rapid succession came the climactic struggle of Jesus' life—in the crucifixion, where his obedience to God won the day; in the resurrection, where the powers of the underworld were smashed; and in the ascension, where he was exalted to a position above all Satanic power and authority.

Blow after blow Christ struck, and time after time Satan came reeling off the ropes to fight again. We too feel his punches in the temptations that beset us and the wickedness that surrounds us.

That is why we need the revelation that the millennium will bring. There Satan's defeat is painted vividly: Heavenly power will bring it about; that is what the angel signifies. Satan's might will be sharply curtailed; that is what the key, the chain, the pit, the seal signify. Figure upon figure make clear that for a thousand years Christ's glory will shine from sea to sea and pole to pole, untarnished by Satan's opposition. Evil will not win. Christ will.

The millennium also points to the finality of

Christ's triumph over Satan. Again John's words in Revelation are gripping:

> And when the thousand years are ended, Satan will be loosed from his prison and will come out to deceive the nations which are at the four corners of the earth . . . to gather them for battle; their number is like the sane of the sea. And they marched up over the broad earth and surrounded the camp of the saints and the beloved city; but fire came down from heaven and consumed them, and the devil who had deceived them was thrown into the lake of fire and sulphur where the beast [antichrist] and the false prophet were, and they will be tormented day and night for ever and ever. (Rev 20:7-10)

The defeat of Satan is overwhelming—who can fight fire from heaven? The fate of Satan is insufferable—what could be greater pain than to be engulfed in a lake of fire? The judgment of Satan is unending—what could be more intolerable than suffering night and day forever? No respite, no relief, no escape: Satan's defeat is final. Evil will not win in the end.

What Is Righteousness Really Like?

The millennium answers another basic question. It gives prolonged opportunity for the human family to see righteousness at work. Think of how tainted and mixed human experience is. Our conduct, both politically and personally, is at best not all that it should be, and at worst much that it should not be. Corruption and contamination ribbon our lives. We never get a full look at what righteousness is really like.

The millennium will be a display of personal righteousness. Christ's people, who have overcome the temptations of antichrist and who have been transformed by resurrection, will be present in wholeness and perfection (Rev 20:4). Free from corruption, cleansed of all impurity, renewed in obedience, the saints will help Christ rule the world. These sons and daughters of God will daily demonstrate what human life should be in love and worship.

The millennium will also demonstrate political righteousness. Remember the context. Antichrist, the vicious beast, has had his infamous fling. His attempts at world rule have worked oppression, cruelty and bondage. For a substantial period of time, perhaps three and a half years, during the Great Tribulation antichrist was given freedom to wreak untold havoc. The political and economic structures were all warped to suit his purposes. It was as though all the evils of all the bad governments of history had combined in one explosion of wickedness.

Christ's coming had destroyed antichrist and broken his political stranglehold on the nations of the world. Then came the millennium in John's vision of future history. And with the millennium came the righteous reign of Christ. What a contrast! No oppression, no exploitation, no manipulation, no injustice! For once a government will do the will of God on earth as it is done in heaven. Executing justice, relieving oppression, caring for the underprivileged, Christ will demonstrate once for all in his reign what righteousness is really like.

Is Judgment Truly Fair?

Questions about righteousness and victory are basic. But the most fundamental questions may have to do with judgment and its fairness. So much in life seems arbitrary. We find little correlation between what *should* happen and what *does* happen. A helicopter crashes at a church picnic and a joyful game turns into a bloody massacre. Some of the best people we know are struck down early by accident or disease, while the mean and selfish may live for a century.

Will life ever even out? Will people really get what they deserve? Will God's justice ultimately make sense?

The millennium helps to answer such questions by exposing human unbelief. The picture is almost incredible. Christ and his resurrected people rule the world in righteousness for ten centuries; yet at the close of that reign, when Satan is loosed, huge sections of the human family follow him: "Their number is like the sand of the sea" (Rev 20:8). Their persistent unbelief in the face of Christ's righteousness confirms the words of his parable: "If they do not hear Moses and the prophets, neither will they be convinced if some one should rise from the dead" (Lk 16:31). The risen Christ stood among them, beside him a vast multitude of the saints risen from the dead in the first resurrection. Yet the nations believed the lies of Satan, not the reality of resurrection. What can God do but judge such unbelief?

The millennium helps also to answer questions of God's justice by uncovering human rebellion. A thousand years of righteousness give way to an act of insurrection. Armies impelled by Satan march against God's people and his city, Jerusalem. God himself has to intervene to defeat them. Can there be any clearer picture of human perversity? What can God do but judge such rebellion?

Some questions, like those of ultimate victory, perfect righteousness and just judgment, can be answered only by God himself living and working among us. Thanks to his holy Scripture we do not have to wait for the millennium to learn the answers. Before that time, with hope and faith, we can rejoice in that victory, live for that righteousness and warn others of that judgment. And the God of millennial glory will help us as we do.

Then I saw a great white throne and him who sat upon it; from his presence earth and sky fled away, and no place was found for them. And I saw the dead, great and small, standing before the throne, and books were opened. Also another book was opened, which is the book of life. And the dead were judged by what was written in the books, by what they had done. And the sea gave up the dead in it, Death and Hades gave up the dead in them, and all were judged by what they had done. Then Death and Hades were thrown into the lake of fire. This is the second death, the lake of fire; and if any one's name was not found written in the book of life, he was thrown into the lake of fire.
Revelation 20:11-15

9
The Second Resurrection

SOME OF THE most important teachings of the Bible are hard to believe. So it seems to millions in our modern generation. They have adopted as a theme song the lines from *Porgy and Bess*, "It ain't necessarily so."

A few cynics who question the teachings of Scripture are consistent. They reject everything that the Bible says—whether about God, afterlife, ethical obligation or the spiritual aspects of our human nature. According to their outlook, we are animals, the last accidents in a mindless venture of evolution, products of a process beyond our control, destined for extinction or gradual change by adaptation. Religious expressions are but expressions of insecurity. Morals are but convenient customs, practiced to enhance our animal existence. Afterlife is but a fiction forged by the human imagination to make death more palatable.

Other skeptics are less consistent. They admire the religious values and moral concerns of the Bible without accepting its supernatural picture of reality. Prayer, they might say, is good therapy; it gives religious people a chance to get things off their chests. Morality as taught in the Bible is an excellent description of the best in human conduct, like the ethics of Plato and Kant or the philosophies of Confucius. But as for God and the devil, sin and final judgment, resurrection to a destiny in heaven or hell—these skeptics will have nothing to do with them.

Probably even more common is the sentimental skeptic who believes the "good parts" of what the Bible teaches and doubts the rest. A recent survey by Andrew Greeley, a priest and sociologist, claims that seventy per cent of Roman Catholics believe in heaven but only thirty-three per cent believe in hell. Martin Marty, a historian from the University of Chicago, notes that only one person in eight who believes in hell believes hell is a threat to him. And Neil Warren, former dean of the Graduate School of Psychology at Fuller Seminary, reports that he almost never hears his patients speak of fearing judgment, even though death is a subject frequently discussed.

Hell is the terrible things that happen to us in this life: so goes the popular strain of opinion, sometimes reinforced by the teachings of so-called Christian religions. Belief in hell has also been called into question by recent reports on what people experience when they are near death. Raymond Moody's book *Life after Life* contains numerous such reports. Frequently the dying describe their journey from the body as including a reunion with loved ones and a vision of a being of light, light which felt warm and loving and which drew them to it. No one has reported to Dr. Moody an experience which sounds like the biblical picture of hell, although Dr. Moody is quick to add, "Nothing I have encountered precludes the possibility of hell" (*Los Angeles Times,* 21 August 1978, 1, 3, 14).

According to Scripture, however, there will be a second resurrection which will be followed by God's final judgment of all unbelievers. The picture in the Revelation is too plain to be interpreted any other way than as a climactic, calamitous event yet to come:

> Then I saw a great white throne and him who sat upon it; from his presence earth and sky fled away, and no place was found for them. And I saw the dead, great and small, standing before the throne, and books were opened. Also another book was opened, which is the book of life. And the dead were judged by what was written in the books, by what they had done. And the sea gave up the dead in it, Death and Hades gave up the dead in them, and all were judged by what they had done. Then Death and Hades were thrown into the lake of fire. This is the second death, the lake of fire; and if any one's

name was not found written in the book of life,
he was thrown into the lake of fire. (Rev 20:11-15)
Two great lessons crowd to the front in this drama
of the second resurrection: human life is more than
physical, and divine judgment is beyond escape.
Understanding these lessons will help us come to
grips with the doctrine of hell as an important
aspect of Christian teaching.

Human Life Is More Than Physical

Why the scene of judgment with its risen dead, its
opened books, its shining throne? Why disturb the
bodies long buried at sea? Why empty the graves
of their dusty remains?

Because human life is more than physical. This
final resurrection of the dead announces that. It
tells us that we are not animals whose destiny is to
lie forever in the dust, at one with the material
world. We, as those who bear God's image in our
nature, have to live eternally with the implications
of who we are and what we have done.

Though death takes us all, it is not the great
leveler. It is the great divider. It marks off those
who have trusted Christ from those who have not.
It makes permanent the loyalty we have pledged to
God or the rebellion we have mounted against him.
But it does its dividing in secret. No clinical chart
can record whether the departing person is going
to be with God or elsewhere. No autopsy can measure a corpse's final destiny. That most basic question is left unanswered to the wondering gaze of
all who watch death do its work.

What death has kept secret, the second resurrection (predicted in Revelation 20:5) will reveal. The spiritual natures of the human family—so set in opposition to God, so calloused to his claims on their lives—will be reunited with resurrected bodies. Then the whole person, made by and for and like God, will be judged by the righteous Creator.

What death itself could not accomplish, the second resurrection will bring to finality. Though death itself is a form of punishment, it is not thorough enough, just enough, nor final enough to do what human rebellion merits. Sin is not just physical. We are spiritual creatures, and our sin has spiritual expressions. Most important, our sin has eternal consequences because it is rejection of the eternal God. If the punishment is to fit the crime, then death is not enough. Beyond death must come resurrection and judgment.

Human life is more than physical. The terrifying picture of that one, last, inclusive, total, final judgment shouts that lesson to us. Pity those so stubborn, so foolish, as not to believe it!

Divine Judgment Is beyond Escape
Inescapable—that word jolts our very souls as we look at John's mural of resurrection and judgment. Every detail in the painting conspires to confront us with its unavoidable reality. Human life is more than physical—that is the first great lesson of the drama. The second is equally clear, fully as forceful: divine judgment is beyond escape.

God's judgment is so awesome that the elements flee from it. "From his presence earth and sky fled away, and no place was found for them" (Rev

20:11). The throne is great, overwhelming in its massiveness; the throne is white, formidable in its radiance; the throne is occupied by God, unbearable in his glory. The awesomeness of the scene causes the most massive and permanent things we know, earth and sky, to flee from the stage and to look for shelter in the wings: "and no place was found for them." God's pervasive glory in resurrection and judgment is too much for them. If they cannot hide, how can any sinner escape?

Besides, the earth and the sky know that their time has come. The second resurrection is the last great event before the new creation comes into being, with a new heaven and a new earth. The old elements are in retreat. The renewing power of God who says, "Behold, I make all things new" is already at work (Rev 21:5). In awe and reverence, the old earth and the ancient sky bow out of the picture.

God's judgment is awesome and sweeping, so sweeping that all of the dead are included in it: "And I saw the dead, great and small, standing before the throne.... And the sea gave up the dead in it, Death and Hades gave up the dead in them, and all were judged by what they had done" (Rev 20:12-13). Prominent or obscure, buried at sea or on land—all of those not raised in the first resurrection were brought from the dead by the power of him who sits on the throne (Rev 20:4-5). The Creator again took dust and breathed life into it, and living souls stood before him for judgment.

To be human is to be accountable to God. He made us for his purposes. He will call us to account for those purposes and how we have fulfilled them. No person from any age or continent can escape the sweeping accountability of that judgment.

God's judgment is awesome, sweeping and accurate, so accurate that no appeal can be made against it. That is what we learn from the description of the books: "And books were opened. Also another book was opened, which is the book of life. And the dead were judged by what was written in the books" (Rev 20:12). The judgment is not arbitrary. It is based on records of our conduct, particularly the record of our acceptance of God's gift of eternal life through Jesus: "And if any one's name was not found written in the book of life, he was thrown into the lake of fire" (Rev 20:15).

When we come to these verses, the millennium with all its glory has ended. During the thousand years of Christ's rule, many will come to trust him, especially many of Israel's sons and daughters. Their names are in the book of life. They are welcomed into full fellowship with all of God's people. The others, including those who joined Satan's final burst of revolution, are not named in that book of grace and life (Rev 20:7-9). They have not been redeemed by Christ's death and resurrection. They have to face their deeds—and the consequences of them.

With detailed accuracy they are found wanting and sentenced to separation from God and his people. The great white throne is history's highest court. Its verdict is incontestably final. There will be no arguing over evidence, no quibbling over procedures, no outrage over the decision. The gavel will descend and all humanity will yield to its irreversible verdict.

God's judgment is awesome, sweeping, accurate and final, so final that even Death and Hades are no longer needed: "Then Death and Hades were thrown into the lake of fire. This is the second death, the lake of fire" (Rev 20:14). This is a picture too vivid to look at without shielding the eyes.

God's program of judgment and salvation is racing toward its climax in the new heaven and earth. The equipment of this life and this earth is ready for discarding. Death and Hades speak of the grave, that temporary means of judgment which God has used throughout human history to remind us of our frailty, our dependence on him, our accountability to him. They have done their work and are destroyed along with everything else not needed in the new age. The inescapable judgment is complete, and God is readying the universe for its total redemption.

Some of the Bible's most important teaching seems hard to believe. But we will miss what God is like, where history is going and how accountable we are, unless we hear the message of the second resurrection—and heed what we hear.

Then I saw a new heaven and a new earth; for the first heaven and the first earth had passed away, and the sea was no more. And I saw the holy city, new Jerusalem, coming down out of heaven from God, prepared as a bride adorned for her husband; and I heard a loud voice from the throne saying, "Behold, the dwelling of God is with men. He will dwell with them, and they shall be his people, and God himself will be with them; he will wipe away every tear from their eyes, and death shall be no more, neither shall there be mourning nor crying nor pain any more, for the former things have passed away."

And he who sat upon the throne said, "Behold, I make all things new." Also he said, "Write this, for these words are trustworthy and true." And he said to me, "It is done! I am the Alpha and the Omega, the beginning and the end. To the thirsty I will give from the fountain of the water of life without payment. He who conquers shall have this heritage, and I will be his God and he shall be my son."
Revelation 21:1-7

10

The New Heaven and Earth

ENTROPY IS NOT a word that most of us use regularly. But it is an important word because it describes what scientists say is happening to our universe. Entropy, according to *Webster's New Collegiate Dictionary*, is "the degradation of the matter and energy in the universe to an ultimate state of inert uniformity." To use the popular definition, entropy is the process by which the universe is gradually running down or wearing out.

"An ultimate state of inert uniformity": that is the destiny of our universe as defined by the laws of thermodynamics. All that scientists know about the relationship of matter and energy has us headed in that direction, though the process is scheduled to take millions of years. What a contrast between "inert uniformity" and what the Bible promises about the future of our world!

Renewal, not entropy, is the biblical prediction. It is described in some of Scripture's most moving language:

> Then I saw a new heaven and a new earth; for the first heaven and the first earth had passed away, and the sea was no more. And I saw the holy city, new Jerusalem, coming down out of heaven from God, prepared as a bride adorned for her husband; and I heard a loud voice from the throne saying, "Behold, the dwelling of God is with men. He will dwell with them, and they shall be his people, and God himself will be with them; he will wipe away every tear from their eyes, and death shall be no more, neither shall there be mourning nor crying nor pain any more, for the former things have passed away." (Revelation 21:1-4)

Entropy, yes! The former things *will* pass away. Entropy as the universe's final destiny, no! Three great realities about the future leap from John's vision in the Revelation—the realities of the creation restored, the fellowship renewed and the blessings bestowed. Among the substantial benefits of Christ's second coming, they are the assurance that God's whole program of salvation is to be accomplished.

The Creation Restored

To the people of the Bible salvation is a broad, not

a narrow, concept. It deals not just with the rescue of individuals nor even with the forming of a people. It reaches out to embrace the whole creation, which was spoken into existence by God's word at the beginning and which was defiled by our human rebellion. It is as though God's creation were an ensemble, no part of which can truly play its music until every instrument is in tune. Salvation —the total event of God's deliverance—is not complete until the enemies, like the antichrist and Satan, death and sorrow, are totally eliminated. They have played their discordant notes throughout the whole score of human history; they have marred the harmonies of God's symphony from just after the beginning to the final clashing chords. Then, just before the end, the master Conductor will purify the orchestra, wipe out the discordant instruments and tune the whole ensemble to play his richest, finest strains for all eternity.

"Then I saw a new heaven and a new earth; for the first heaven and the first earth had passed away" (Rev 21:1). This is the completion of a scene begun in the previous chapter, where John "saw a great white throne and him who sat upon it; from his presence earth and sky fled away, and no place was found for them" (Rev 20:11). The old order, in which Satan did his work as prince of earth and air, has passed away, driven from the presence of God by his awesome glory. And the new era has begun —a totally new creation, expressed in terms of a new heaven and a new earth.

It is a picture of full provision. Just as the first heaven and earth whose creation was summarized in Genesis 1 provided all that the human family needed for its pleasure, work and sustenance, so the new creation will make that full provision. All that God's people will need to live joyfully through all eternity will be available to them in the new creation.

It is a picture of full security as well. One specific feature of the new heaven and earth is that "the sea was no more" (Rev 21:1). To the people of the Bible the sea was an enemy. God had to cleave it in two at the Exodus when he led Israel through the Sea of Reeds. Solomon had to hire Phoenicians to run his fleet because the people of Judah had no seafaring skills and no interest in learning them; the sea was too threatening an environment for them to call home. Jesus, demonstrating in his miracles the power of the new age, both calmed the sea and walked on the waters. He thoroughly tamed the ancient enemy.

God will keep his loved ones secure. The turbulent, restless, changing, overwhelming sea will be no more. John, who had been cut off from his loved ones during his captivity on the island of Patmos, must have hated the sea that formed such a barrier. The vision of no more sea must have been especially comforting to him.

Provision and security will mark the world when the creation is restored by God's irresistible power. Not entropy but restoration is creation's destiny.

The Fellowship Renewed

John's vision of the new heaven and earth was glorious in itself, but it was just the beginning. As he watched God's future unfold before his eyes, he "saw the holy city, new Jerusalem, coming down out of heaven from God, prepared as a bride adorned for her husband" (Rev 21:2). John did not have to ponder the scene long. From God's own throne came the explanation: "Behold, the dwelling of God is with men. He will dwell with them, and they shall be his people, and God himself will be with them" (Rev 21:3).

The new age will bring not only cosmic changes as the creation is restored, but also personal changes as God's fellowship with his people is renewed. The first part of John's vision centers in the prepared dwelling. Jerusalem, from the time of David on, was seen as the dwelling place of God. The Temple was there and so was the ark of the covenant, the special symbol of his presence. Shrouded by the radiant cloud that the Jews called *Shekinah*, the ark was so holy that only the high priest could stand before it, and that just once a year.

The holy city, the new Jerusalem, then, pictures the dwelling place of God descending from heaven to earth. The direction is significant and so is the destination. The direction is downward. It is not an old Jerusalem rebuilt on earth by human hands, but a new Jerusalem coming down from heaven. Salvation from beginning to end is God's doing. It is heavenly work. It does not spring up from earth to heaven as the Tower of Babel tried to do; it descends from God to our humanity.

The destination of the new Jerusalem is earth. God has come to make his eternal dwelling with us. The earth that God called good in the beginning he has now restored and called good again, so good that he is willing to dwell with us here. Our biblical faith is not an escape from the material world. Its final destiny is not an ethereal existence where floating spirits circle a heavenly throne. The Bible's last pictures show God on earth entering into fellowship with a resurrected people who live a bodily, human existence.

We see the beauty and completeness of this fellowship in the words "prepared as a bride adorned for her husband" (Rev 21:2). God has left no detail untended. No loose ends mar the scene. As a bride and her family spare no pains to see that she arrives at the wedding sparklingly groomed and faultlessly dressed, so God's new dwelling is free from all flaws. Think of the radiance. Nothing is more characteristic of an eager, hopeful bride than a glorious glow that flames from within to light and warm all who see her. What a picture to be awaited and welcomed—God's dwelling prepared for him and his people on earth!

In a sense, the prepared dwelling is the setting for something even more welcome: the permanent covenant. Permanence is a new element. God's first dwelling with Israel was in a tent that could be moved from place to place. On at least one occasion the ark of his dwelling was pirated by the Philistines and carted off to their cities, outside Judah's boundaries. The Temple, where God dwelt after Solomon's time, was destroyed by the Babylonians. But even before its destruction Ezekiel envisaged its glory's departing as part of God's judgment on his wayward people (Ezek 10—11). When in Jesus "the Word became flesh and dwelt [or tented] among us," we indeed experienced the very presence of God (Jn 1:14). But even that was temporary—about thirty-three short years. Then Jesus ascended to the Father's side.

John's vision marked the coming of a new day. A city coming down, God with his people on earth, a covenant of full fellowship instigated: these are pictures of permanence. We can rejoice in them now and long for their rapid fulfillment.

The language emphasizes the wonder of the covenant: "And they shall be his [God's] people, and God himself will be with them" (Rev 21:3). These words echo the vows of an ancient wedding ceremony, where each party would pledge to belong to the other, the husband to the wife, the wife to the husband. Our future fellowship, rich and permanent, is guaranteed by God's own promise. The material world may be captured in the grips of entropy, energy and matter wearing out in the whirl of prolonged activity. But God's people are headed for the renewal that permanent fellowship with him will produce.

The Blessings Bestowed

With that renewal come special blessings. This is what we should expect. The old Jerusalem promised blessings to all who with clean hands and pure heart ascended the holy mount to the Temple: "He will receive blessing from the LORD, and vindication from the God of his salvation" (Ps 24:5).

The blessings of the new Jerusalem are described this way: "He will wipe away every tear from their eyes, and death shall be no more, neither shall there be mourning nor crying nor pain any more, for the former things have passed away" (Rev 21:4). Rather than list all possible blessings, the voice from the throne focused on the one indispensable blessing, the one great gift which truly captures the newness of the new Jerusalem—the absence of death and its tragic effects.

The agelong chain of death and grief has been snapped. Death itself, along with Hades, was thrown into the lake of fire (Rev 20:14). No longer will death claim us as victims. Its work has been done; its power has been crushed; its captives have been freed. God dwells with his people, and death, with the tears that it induces, has no place in his presence. Vibrant, pulsating life—not inertia, not entropy—is the mood of the new age.

All this is by God: "And he who sat upon the throne said, 'Behold, I make all things new' " (Rev 21:5). Its renewal is not just modification or re-adjustment. It will have a freshness as startling as God's first defeat of chaos at the beginning. It is new *creation* to the last detail. All the limiting, compromising, threatening aspects of the old creation are put aside. The truly new has come as God alone can make it come.

All this is true: "Also [God] said, 'Write this, for these words are trustworthy and true' " (Rev 21:5). God is the surety for the truth of this picture. No imagined utopia, no fanciful Shangri-la, no imagined planet of science fiction—this new age to which we press, in which by faith we already live, is as real as God himself.

All this is satisfying: "It is done! I am the Alpha and the Omega, the beginning and the end. To the thirsty I will give from the fountain of the water of life without payment" (Rev 21:6). God, who is life's beginning and end, will meet the needs of each of his people. His program is cosmic, embracing a new heaven and earth; it is corporate, expressing itself in a holy city, a vast community of people. Yet that program is personal, wiping tears from each eye, refreshing each person with eternal life, free and abundant.

The verdict of science is undoubtedly right: the vast universe of matter and energy is running down. But God's Word is even more right. Creation is headed for restoration; fellowship with God will be renewed in permanence; blessings will be bestowed in abundance. As God's people we lead full lives now. Think what it will be like then.

And I saw no temple in the city, for its temple is the Lord God the Almighty and the Lamb. And the city has no need of sun or moon to shine upon it, for the glory of God is its light, and its lamp is the Lamb. By its light shall the nations walk; and the kings of the earth shall bring their glory into it, and its gates shall never be shut by day—and there shall be no night there; they shall bring into it the glory and the honor of the nations. But nothing unclean shall enter it, nor any one who practices abomination or falsehood, but only those who are written in the Lamb's book of life.

Then he showed me the river of the water of life, bright as crystal, flowing from the throne of God and of the Lamb through the middle of the street of the city; also, on either side of the river, the tree of life with its twelve kinds of fruit, yielding its fruit each month; and the leaves of the tree were for the healing of the nations. There shall no more be anything accursed, but the throne of God and of the Lamb shall be in it, and his servants shall worship him; they shall see his face, and his name shall be on their foreheads. And night shall be no more; they need no light of lamp or sun, for the Lord God will be their light, and they shall reign for ever and ever.

Revelation 21:22—22:5

II
The Eternal Kingdom

THE NEW TESTAMENT'S story begins in a small town and ends in a magnificent city. Bethlehem and the new Jerusalem seem a long way apart. Nearly two thousand years have passed since the carpenter from Nazareth took his pregnant peasant wife to their ancestral city to register in the census. Yet the towns of the world seem much more to resemble the crowded, selfish streets of Bethlehem than the righteous glory of the holy city which John saw in Revelation.

Two cities could hardly be more different. Bethlehem's crude bricks and rough stones bear little resemblance to the jasper walls and golden streets of the future dwelling place of God's people. Yet the two cities are intimately connected.

David's hometown in the hills of Judah covered a few acres and housed a few hundred people. The city where God will live measures fifteen hundred miles square, a splendid edifice worthy to be capital of the universe. Yet without Bethlehem and its manger, the new Jerusalem and its throne would be an impossibility. And no understanding of Christmas can be complete without seeing its connection with those final scenes in the Revelation. What God had at heart when he came to us at Bethlehem is fulfilled to perfection in the new Jerusalem.

That simple town so long ago is like the garden plot in which were sown the seeds of the universal and eternal kingdom of God. In gardening and farming, wrinkled seeds lead to flourishing harvests. So it is in the kingdom of God. Mud brick led to streets of gold. A handful of shepherds prepared the way for a multitude of saints. A manger was refashioned into a throne. A peasant's baby became Lord of the universe.

How much history had to be altered, how thoroughly heaven and earth had to be renewed, to make such changes possible! Everything not under God's rule had to be put down or set aside. Everything temporary had to be discarded. Everything partial had to be made whole for the new Jerusalem to be fit for God's earthly habitation. As we look at the final paragraphs of the Revelation, we see what God will do so that his kingdom can be universal and eternal.

The Barriers Are Leveled

The world at Jesus' birth was crosshatched with barriers. Gentiles were separated from Jews. The Jewish faith demanded this. Those who had entered into covenant with the God of Abraham and Moses had marked that covenant by the act of circumcision. That simple operation separated those who sought to love the Lord with their whole heart from those who worshiped elements of nature—like sun, moon and stars—or idols of wood and stone. Pagans, idolators, lawbreakers—that was how the Jews labeled the Gentiles. Jews would not eat with Gentiles; they would not allow friendships to develop with Gentiles; they certainly would not tolerate intermarriage.

So went the bitter struggle for centuries. Then came Jesus. From the beginning his coming made a difference. Gentile wise men came to worship him. A Samaritan woman was transformed by his words. Greeks came to yield to his lordship. His apostles, especially Paul, took the news of Christ's salvation around the Mediterranean, and Gentiles by the thousands became Christian believers.

Yet in many situations, even among those who professed to be Christians, the barriers persisted over the years. And on some tragic occasions the boundaries between Jews and gentile Christians became battlegrounds. The horrors of the Spanish inquisitions or the Nazi holocaust dramatized the conflict between those who called themselves Christians and their Jewish neighbors.

One of the marks of Christ's universal and eternal kingdom is the leveling of this barrier. Jews and Gentiles hand in hand, side by side, will enjoy true fellowship as God's people. This fellowship is symbolized in the picture of the new Jerusalem which comes from heaven to earth as the place where God will dwell with his people. The twelve gates of that city bear the names of the tribes of Israel; the twelve foundations are inscribed with the names of the Christian apostles (Rev 21:12-14). The old people of God, Israel, and the new people of God, the church, comprised largely of Gentiles, dwell together in the new city. Fellowship, not separation, is the permanent way of life in that final kingdom that Christ will build.

The most forbidding barrier in history, however, is not the wall between Jews and Gentiles, as imposing as that is, but the barrier between us and God. The whole human family was separated from God. That gulf, dug by Adam and Eve when they pitted their will against God's, was unbridgeable from the human side. In fact, our human race much preferred to fashion our own gods and try to please them rather than to come to terms with the living, true God.

In the end, however, it will be God's persistent grace, not our desires, that will prevail. When God called Abraham to follow him, when he sent Jesus to rescue us, he took the task of salvation into his own hands. How well he accomplished it can be seen in those final pictures of Revelation: "And I saw no temple in the city, for its temple is the Lord God the Almighty and the Lamb" (Rev 21:22).

We catch the contrast between this scene and the rest of biblical history. In the early periods people like Abraham and Sarah or Isaac and Rebekah prayed to God and offered sacrifices at their shrines or altars. Later God's people prayed at the tabernacle and, later still, at Solomon's Temple. The details of these worship centers were designed meticulously. The worship was carefully regulated by divine law, and threats of punishment hung heavily on persons who tampered with those regulations.

In the new kingdom all will be different. No altar, no shrine, no tabernacle, no Temple. The center of worship and fellowship will be the Father and the Son, the Lord and the Lamb.

Not even the coming of Christ to Bethlehem can match that. For thirty years or more he dwelt among us. Then he returned to the Father, and the human family saw him no more. Often God seemed remote, unavailable. We have sought him in private prayer and in church worship, but often we have felt unsure of his presence and care. Even the voice of the Spirit within us who trust Christ as Lord seems sometimes muffled, unclear. But that great future: what will it be like? No physical temple, no tangible altar, no ritual or regulation—just worship in spirit and truth, just fellowship and adoration, unhampered by doubt, sin, distance, despair.

Bethlehem began the leveling of barriers. It brought good news of great joy to all people, Jew and Gentile. And it promised that God would be with us. The Child's very name said it: Immanuel. But Bethlehem was only a shadow of that later city, the new Jerusalem. There all barriers are leveled.

All of Christ's people, Jew and Gentile, will rejoice in full fellowship with each other. Even more wondrous, all of Christ's people will have constant access to their living Lord in that kingdom, universal and eternal.

The Elements Are Abandoned

God used a star to guide the wise men to Bethlehem. From creation forward he had used the sun, moon and stars to light day and night and to mark days, months, seasons, years. Genesis records the original divine command: "And let them be lights in the firmament of the heavens to give light upon the earth" (Gen 1:15). As long as God was in heaven, such light for earth was absolutely essential. It divided our calendars, nourished our crops and brightened our footsteps.

In the kingdom yet to come, all this will be unnecessary: "And the city has no need of sun or moon to shine upon it, for the glory of God is its light, and its lamp is the Lamb" (Rev 21:23). This is a dramatic description of the life-giving, light-shedding character of God. His presence renders the essential nonessential; his glory dispenses with what we call indispensable. It boggles the imagination—life without the natural elements that have brightened and blessed human existence since the beginning. What more dramatic way could there be to show how glorious and vital the presence of God really is? When we live in the fullness of that presence, all other light becomes unnecessary. The elements themselves—the sun, moon and stars—can be abandoned.

The Opposition Is Vanquished

Bethlehem's story had more to it than surprised shepherds and devout wise men. It was scarred from the first by conflict. Galilee and Judea were under foreign rule. Their gentle hills reeled under the tramp of Roman boots. The very edict that sent Joseph and Mary toward Bethlehem to be registered was issued by a pagan king. Conflict loomed even larger in Herod's madness as he massacred Jewish toddlers in his vicious plot to kill the Christ.

Through the centuries this malicious opposition to God's program has continued. From Nero to Hitler, from Diocletian to Mao Zedong, the kings of the earth have opposed the salvation of God, a salvation which led humanity to worship God, not the king.

But in the new Jerusalem life will be different. All opposition will be vanquished: "By its light shall the nations walk; and the kings of the earth shall bring their glory into it, and its gates shall never be shut by day—and there shall be no night there; they shall bring into it the glory and the honor of the nations" (Rev 21:24-26). No hostile kings, only nations that seek to glorify God. No forbidding gates, only ready access to all who honor God's presence and God's people.

Sin and Death Are Defeated

The landscape around Bethlehem was marred by the sight of sin and death. Like every other place on our crowded planet, it had been tainted by human rebellion and its damning consequences. That was why Christ came. Dealing with Bethlehem's sin and death was his mission. His own name, Jesus, spelled out his purpose: to save his people from their sin and its death-dealing consequence. His cross and empty tomb were the arena where that salvation was achieved.

Along the way we have tasted the fruit of that salvation. Our sins have been forgiven, our fear of death assuaged. But the fullness of that salvation will only be enjoyed when sin is banished and death defeated. What a picture of relief and victory!

> But nothing unclean shall enter it [the new Jerusalem], nor any one who practices abomination or falsehood, but only those who are written in the Lamb's book of life.
>
> Then he showed me the river of the water of life, bright as crystal, flowing from the throne of God and of the Lamb; . . . also, on either side of the river, the tree of life with its twelve kinds of fruit, yielding its fruit each month; and the leaves of the tree were for the healing of the nations. (Rev 21:27—22:2)

The scene resounds with notes of life: a river with the water of life, expressing the constant refreshment of God's presence; a tree of life, symbolizing the power of God to heal the wounds of history and bring his full salvation. Death and sin have more than met their match. The King has conquered them. Their reign has been swallowed up by his.

All that Bethlehem began has come to fullness. The little town was the seed from which the full-blown city blossomed. And with what fragrance and brilliance!

When Jesus Christ returns we will enter the final phase of history that culminates in the eternal kingdom. Worship of God without impurity, vision of God without concealment, relationship with God without conflict, rulership of God without ending —these are the fruit of that kingdom. With eagerness we anticipate them. By faith in Jesus Christ we can begin to experience them now.